THE GUIDE TO
SALT-WATER
FISHING

THE GUIDE TO SALT-WATER FISHING

MARTIN FORD

CONSULTANT EDITOR BRUCE VAUGHAN

LORENZ BOOKS

This edition published in 2001 by Lorenz Books

Lorenz Books is an imprint of Anness Publishing Limited
Hermes House, 88-89 Blackfriars Road, London SE1 8HA

Published in the USA by Lorenz Books
Anness Publishing Inc., 27 West 20th Street, New York, NY 10011

www.lorenzbooks.com

Distributed in Canada by Raincoast Books
9050 Shaughnessy Street, Vancouver, British Columbia V6P 6E5

A CIP catalogue record for this book is available from the British Library

Publisher: Joanna Lorenz
Project Editor: Doreen Palamartschuk
Editor: Anthony Atha
Designer: James Lawrence
Special Photography: Peter Gathercole, Sue Ford
Illustrators: Mike Atkinson (species)
Dave Batten (rigs and diagrams)
Production Controller: Don Campaniello

Also published as part of a larger compendium,
The Practical Fishing Encyclopedia

1 3 5 7 9 10 8 6 4 2

Contents

Introduction

Sea angling, both from the shore and from a boat, offers great variety and excitement, whether you want to challenge the sporting qualities of bass or partake in a night-time fight with a rough ground conger eel. The successful angler will have to learn and master the techniques of distance casting, experiment to find the best baits and tackle and will, no doubt, fish through many nights on beaches hoping for a catch. But for many sea anglers, big fish are the main target, and plenty of conger eels, ling and pollack can be caught from all manner of wrecks and reefs offshore.

ABOVE: A fishing expedition puts out to sea from a crowded harbour in southern England. Sea fishing is a big tourist attraction in many coastal resorts.

Where to Fish

Sea fishing can be divided into two parts: boat fishing and fishing from the shore. Shore fishing itself can be divided into fishing from marks, harbours and piers, and fishing from the beach. This division may be somewhat artificial as many of the techniques are the same but there can be differences in the species targeted.

The first thing the sea angler has to learn is the type of fish that lives in each habitat. Fishing from a pier or harbour can produce a number of species, but dogfish, garfish, mackerel and mullet can all be caught from harbours, and the beginner has to learn to target each of these species. If you have a rocky coastline available to you then you may well be able to spin for bass and catch pollack, pouting, wrasse, whiting and bream, even the occasional conger eel, while if you live near sandy beaches or on an estuary your quarry will be flounders, dabs and plaice, with codling the target in the winter months. Fish change their habitats during the season, and if you are lucky enough to be able to enjoy access to the sea all the year round then you can fish for different species at different times of the year.

The other things the sea angler has to learn are the technicalities of the

BELOW: The sun slips away as two anglers spin for bass from the shore. Late evening is one of the best times for fish to take.

ABOVE: Sea fishing from a boat on a blissfully calm day in midsummer. A good cod is being brought to the net while the other rod waits for a bite.

craft: what baits to use for each species and how these are best collected; what rods and reels are most effective and what rods suit your purpose. All this takes time.

The sea angler who has access to a boat or belongs to a club that organizes sea-fishing trips has many opportunities. At the top end of the scale many anglers try for shark in the warmer waters of the coasts of Cornwall and Devon in the south-west. If you are a trophy hunter then you may well try and catch a giant thornback ray, now alas present in any quantity only in the seas off the west coast of the Scottish Highlands. Otherwise, children and beginners can have their first chance of success trailing a trace of feathers for mackerel or plumbing the depths to tempt cod or flatfish. As you become more experienced, so you will learn what rigs to use and what baits are most effective, and later you will learn how to reach the wrecks and marks on the sea bed and how these should be fished to best effect.

Sea angling is a fascinating sport. It is limitless in the variety that it offers, both in the number of species that can be caught and the methods that can be used. It is about understanding the way of the tides and species that swim beneath its waters. It is also an endless learning curve, as each day something will change. No two trips, either on shore or in a boat far out to sea, are ever the same, and that above all makes it continuously challenging.

RIGHT: Fishing from a harbour wall in high summer. Many youngsters get their first taste of sea fishing on holidays by the sea.

Species

Garfish *(Belone belone)*

Like a relic from the prehistoric age the garfish, or "green bone" as it is sometimes called, is a real sporting fighter. It is a distant relative of the tropical flying-fish and displays an acrobatic skill of tail walking when hooked. It has the characteristics of a scaled-down swordfish with its protruding, tooth-lined bill, but rarely exceeds 1.5 lb (0.68 kg) in weight.

Long and slim, with a blue-green back and silvery underside, the garfish is often caught in mackerel shoals. Very common around the south-west shores of Britain during the summer months, the garfish likes to feed high up in the water, just below the surface. It will often leap clear from the water when hooked and tail walk across the water in an effort to lose the hook.

For the beginner, the garfish can provide an easy quarry and can be caught from a pier using light float tackle. It is also referred to as the mackerel guard or mackerel guide due to the fact that where there are garfish present, mackerel are always close by.

Current Records
Shore **3 lb 4 oz 12 drm (1.477 kg)**
Boat **3 lb 9 oz 8 drm (1.63 kg)**

Season
April through to October.

Distribution
Widespread but mainly found in the warmer waters of the south-west coast of Britain.

Natural Diet
They are mainly surface feeders, feeding on small fry such as whitebait.

Top Spots
Every pier and breakwater along the south, south-east and south-west coast.

Top Tip
Fish with a light line of 6 lb (2.72 kg) and use a small float with a thin strip of mackerel as bait. This will provide you with a sporting fight as the hooked garfish displays its acrobatic skills.

Conger Eel *(Conger conger)*

Current Records
Shore **68 lb 8 oz (31.072 kg)**
Boat **133 lb 4 oz (60.442 kg) USA**

Season
Can be caught all through the year but June to October is the peak time.

Distribution
All around the British coast, but especially off the southern coastline. Also present in the Atlantic Ocean and North Sea.

Natural Diet
Small species of fish such as pouting and bream, common lobsters, squids and small octopus.

Top Spots
Wrecks off the south and south-west coast.

Top Tip
A freshly caught mackerel head-and-guts bait is one of the most successful known.

Despite its enormous size the conger is a shy, timid creature, which retreats from the slightest sign of danger. However, it is an inquisitive fish and will readily swim out of its lair to search out food. It is a powerful fighting fish and once hooked has the ability to latch on to an obstacle on the bottom if allowed to do so.

Body colourings vary depending on the depth of water in which the conger is caught. Most conger eels are of a dark, smoke-grey colouring along the back with a pale silvery-yellow belly. The dorsal fin of the conger living in deeper water is tipped with a harsh black rim. Their teeth are set in the depths of powerful jaws and are rarely seen. The conger prefers to grip its prey in the clasp of its jaws before taking it into the mouth to be chewed up. When on the move it tends to travel at mid-water depths and when hunting it stays close to the bottom, feeding on smaller fish. Most of the bigger species are caught by boat anglers fishing over deep-water wrecks and reefs. The conger spawns only once in its lifetime, this taking place far away from British shores in deep water near Madeira. A spawning conger will lay up to 15 million eggs, which are carried on the slow-moving currents of the North Atlantic Drift towards the Continental Shelf.

As the larger species are found on wrecks and rough ground, commercial fishing has little effect on the stocks. Big congers in excess of 100 lb (45.36 kg) can therefore thrive in comparative safety. Conger eels caught from the shore tend to be smaller and are mainly caught at night over rough ground and rock-gully marks. At night they move inshore into the shallower water to feed on the abundance of food that these areas attract.

Pouting *(Gadus luscus)*

Sometimes called a bib, the pouting is another member of the cod family and is regarded as a nuisance fish by many sea anglers. This is due to its bait-robbing habits when small. Widespread around British shores, small pouting can be caught in vast numbers when fishing from the beach at night. They don't grow to huge sizes, and the average shore-caught pouting is likely to be under 1 lb (0.45 kg) in weight. Boat anglers are more likely to catch a bigger specimen, and a 3 lb (1.36 kg) pouting is a good fish.

As with the cod, the pouting also has a barbule positioned under the chin. However, it is thinner than that of the cod. It has a sheen of pink in its colouring, which extends from behind the head to the tail, over a coppery-brown back. The underside is pale cream and a black spot can be found at the base of the pectoral fin. Once taken from the water, the pink sheen melts away and the skin turns a dreary copper colour. Pouting spawn in the late winter or early spring, the eggs taking around two weeks to hatch. Smaller pouting will inhabit areas of shore line offering firm sandy beaches and rocky foreshores, even entering estuaries in search of food, while big pouting live in deeper water over rough ground and wrecks. When caught, pouting scales can be difficult to remove from the angler's hands and clothing.

The fish makes an excellent bait for bigger species, such as cod, conger and bass. Each year many thousands of pouting are caught commercially and used to make fishmeal feeds and fertilizers.

Current Records
Shore **4 lb 9 oz (2.07 kg)**
Boat **5 lb 8 oz (2.495 kg)**

Season
All year round.

Distribution
Widely distributed around the British coast, they are most abundant along the south coast.

Natural Diet
Shrimps, swimming crabs, worms, shellfish and squid.

Top Spots
Down the side of pier and breakwater walls, notably Dover Breakwater.

Top Tip
Use short hook snoods when fishing for pouting as they have a habit of spinning in the tide. which often results in a tangled trace.

Cod *(Gadus morrhua)*

The cod is widespread around the coast of Britain, but is particularly found off the coast of Scotland where it comes in from the Icelandic breeding grounds to feed.

Furnished with a large mouth, the cod has a reputation as an eater of all that comes its way. With its pot belly and cylindrical body shape, the cod is not rated highly as a fighting fish. Cod may vary considerably in colour but are usually greeny-brown or olive grey. They will often have a light marbling pattern or spots on the flanks and back. The upper jaw exceeds the lower, which results in a receding chin, upon the underside of which a large barbule is located. Cod are primarily bottom feeders, favouring deep water marks.

Shore anglers in the north can catch cod all year round, but in the south, smaller cod, or codling as they are known, are more of a winter species. The coasts of Kent and Sussex are popular venues for the shore angler in search of prime winter cod fishing. Bigger cod can be caught from the Needles area off the Isle of Wight. Inshore they will search out their food over the rough grounds of rock and pebble beaches at high water, while from a boat they can be located in deep water over wrecks. Being scavengers, they feed on almost anything that comes their way, such as lugworms, prawns, small flatfish, crabs, squid and cuttlefish. Big cod are often caught on artificial eels, pirks or other types of artificial lure.

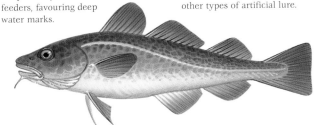

Current Records
Shore **44 lb 8 oz (20.185 kg)**
Boat **58 lb 6 oz (25.572 kg)**
World **98 lb 12 oz (44.79 kg) USA**

Season
January to December in the north, October to February in the south.

Distribution
In northern waters cod are present throughout the year, especially in Scottish waters. During the winter months in the south, venues such as the north coast of Devon can produce good cod fishing.

Natural Diet
Lugworms, cuttlefish, squids, prawns, crabs and small flatfish such as plaice.

Top Spots
Estuary marks, such as the Thames and Bristol Channel, produce good numbers of smaller cod each year. Bigger specimens are to be found from such marks as the Needles and wrecks off the south-west and eastern coasts.

Top Tip
The use of modern braided lines makes cod fishing from a boat much easier. The lack of stretch in the line means that bites are more positive and can be felt by holding the line. This gives the angler an early bite indication.

Tope *(Galeorhinus galeus)*

A member of the shark family, the tope has a reputation as a dogged fighter. Unlike the shark, the tope is a bottom feeder and spends its time searching out food over smooth, sandy, shell-grit bottoms. Sometimes confused with the smoothhound, it is easy to identify by the lack of white dots along its back. It also has serrated, razor-sharp teeth, which the smoothhound lacks. The tope is of a similar shape and build to a shark but is much smaller in size. The body is sleek, with a brownish-grey back and flanks, while the underside is a bright, polished white colour. Positioned behind the head and on the edge of the pectoral fins on each side are five gill slits. Males and females can be distinguished by looking closely at the fins. The male fish have fleshy appendages, known as claspers, alongside the anal fin, which are not present on the female. The female tope gives birth to live young, usually up to 20 at a

time and sometimes as many as 50. The eye is specially adapted, with what is known as a third eyelid: a separate membrane that can be drawn across the eye to clean the eyeball and protect it as it lashes out at its prey.

The average boat-caught tope weighs around 40 lb (18.14 kg). However they do grow in excess of 70 lb (31.75 kg) and are a hard-fighting species once hooked. Tope fishing from the shore tends to result in smaller fish, of around the 20 lb (9.07 kg) mark, that have come into shallower water to feed on small flatfish. The bigger specimens have a tendency to keep to sandy or patchy rough ground found in deeper waters. Highly regarded for their sporting quality, it has become good practice by many sea anglers to return tope to the sea after capture.

Current Records
Shore **58 lb 2 oz (26.366 kg)**
Boat **82 lb 8 oz (37.422 kg)**
World **98 lb 8 oz (44.67 kg) USA**

Season
May through to October, with June and July the most productive months.

Distribution
Spread around the British coast with strongholds off the west coast and the Thames Estuary.

Natural Diet
Tope feed on various bottom-dwelling creatures including starfish and lobsters. The mainstays of their diet are small cod, whiting, flatfish and pouting.

Top Spots
The Thames Estuary, Poole in Dorset, Rhyl in Wales and off Hayling, Sussex.

Top Tip
Mackerel or a fresh eel section make very good tope baits.

Bass *(Dicentrarchus labrax)*

The bass is a member of the perch family and is sometimes referred to as the sea perch. It is coated in small, firm, silvery-blue scales, which give it a striking appearance. It is a predator and the body is muscular and streamlined as it often swims at high speeds when chasing prey. Smaller bass vary in colour and bear a slight resemblance to the mullet. However, they are easily identified by the spikes on their dorsal fin and boney gill covers.

Small school bass, as they are known, can often be caught in estuaries and will make their way right up into the brackish water, and even freshwater, on a rising tide. Once the tide starts to ebb, they follow the flow back towards the sea and feed in earnest on food caught in the tide's fall. Over the past ten years the bass population has suffered severely due to overfishing by commercial fishermen, and nowadays few big

bass are caught from the shore. During the spring and summer months, small bass move inshore to feed in the warmer waters and can be found in good numbers on the south and west coasts of Britain. In the far west country, bass have been known to be caught all year round if the weather stays mild. From time to time bigger species do get caught from shore marks, but as a rule the angler seeking a specimen bass is better advised to fish from a boat. Larger bass tend to be lone fish but will, during stormy weather, move inshore to feed over rocky gullies and around storm beaches. The rough weather and pounding surf will have the bass searching for razor fish and crabs flushed out of their homes by the rough sea.

Current Records
Shore **19 lb (8.618 kg)**
Boat **19 lb 9 oz 2 drm (8.877 kg)**
World **20 lb 11 oz (9.4 kg) France**

Season
May through to October (later if warm).

Distribution
More common around the south-east and west coasts of Britain and Ireland.

Natural Diet
Crustaceans, small shrimps and sandeels. Larger bass are predators and will feed on sprats, squid, crab, mackerel and occasionally sea trout.

Top Spots
The Thames Estuary and Bristol Channel consistently produce double-figure bass.

Top Tip
Try fishing with a live sandeel using minimum weight like a split shot or drilled bullet lead. This will give the sandeel a natural appearance and will not hinder its ability to swim.

Ballan Wrasse *(Labrus bergylta)*

Ballan wrasse are the largest and most common fish of the wrasse family. The ballan has a deep, solid body and a large, long dorsal fin running from behind the head down to the wrist of the tail. The dorsal fin has 20 sharp spiny rays near the top of the back and requires careful handling. The jaws are very powerful, and the rubbery lips and sharp teeth are designed for tearing shellfish from rock faces. The peg-like front teeth are bright white in colour and are only used for tearing. The wrasse grinds its food down with a set of pharyngeal teeth located further back in the mouth. Its colour depends on where it is caught.

The newcomer to sea angling often makes the mistake of wrong identification, because of variations in coloration. In general, the ballan wrasse is of a greenish-brown colour, with the addition of a reddish, fire-orange belly dotted with white spots.

The average size for the ballan wrasse is around 2–3 lb (0.91–1.36 kg); a bigger fish of 7 lb (3.18 kg) is a once-in-a-lifetime catch. Larger fish are commonly found in deeper water, near rocky overhangs and gullies. In the cover of thick kelp weed they can feed at leisure on small crustaceans, such as crabs and lobsters. Smaller ballan wrasse are often caught from breakwater walls and piers and can offer endless sport for the beginner to sea angling as they are relatively easy to catch.

Current Records
Shore **9 lb 1 oz (4.110 kg)**
Boat **9 lb 7 oz 12 drm (4.302 kg)**
World **9 lb 9 oz (4.35 kg) Ireland**

Season
April through to October.

Distribution
Widespread in the British Isles. Bigger specimens are found on the west coast of Britain around the Scillies and Channel Islands. South Cornwall and the south-western coast of Ireland also offer specimen-sized ballans.

Natural Diet
Limpets, common mussels, velvet-swimming crabs, other crustaceans and molluscs.

Top Spot
Alderney in the Channel Islands is famous for producing big wrasse.

Top Tip
Try float fishing or legering a small, hard-backed shore crab for instant results. Look under the rocks and weed near to where you are fishing for crabs about 1 in (2.5 cm) across.

Whiting *(Merlangius merlangus)*

A member of the cod family, the whiting is the most common of sea species to be caught off the British coast. From the shore it is mostly caught throughout the winter months and does not grow to a great size. One look inside the mouth will reveal that the whiting is a predator. It has a protruding upper jaw and an array of small teeth, which it uses to feed on smaller fish close to the sea bed. Colouring on the whiting sometimes leads to confusion for the novice angler, and it is often wrongly identified as a pouting. The whiting has a pinkish-brown sheen across its back and the silver flanks lead to a whitish belly. Some fish have small black dots across the back, but this is not common in all whiting. The whiting spawns between the months of March and June and larger females can lay many thousands of eggs. Growth in the young fish is prolific and it can double its size in two years, reaching 15–18 in (38–45 cm) by the fourth year.

Whiting are more at home in shallower water and are caught from the shore in greater numbers than from a boat. However, boat-caught species tend to be bigger and may reach weights of 3 lb (1.36 kg) and upwards. Towards the end of August the whiting start to move inshore to feed for the winter, and the best sport can be had during late evenings on a high tide from the beach or a pier. Shallow, sandy storm beaches and bays are good places for whiting in the winter.

Current Records
Shore **4 lb 7 drm (1.827 kg)**
Boat **6 lb 12 oz (3.062 kg)**
World **6 lb 13 oz (3.11 kg) Norway**

Season
August through to January.

Distribution
All through the coastal waters of Britain. They are also found in Norway, the North Sea and the English Channel.

Natural diet
The whiting feeds on practically any small fish but especially on sprats.

Top Spot
Both the Norfolk and Suffolk coasts produce good catches, especially around Aldeburgh. Whiting to 4 lb (1.814 kg) can be caught from boats in the English Channel.

Top Tip
Mackerel strip-baited feathers are excellent from a boat, while lugworms tipped with either squid or mackerel strip work best from the shore.

Coalfish *(Pollachius virens)*

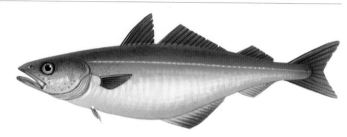

Current Records
Shore **37 lb 5 oz (16.925 kg)**
Boat **24 lb 11 oz 12 drm (11.22 kg)**

Season
September through to March.

Distribution
They are widely distributed around the British coastline, but are more common to the northern waters of Scotland.

Natural Diet
Small fish, herring fry and whitebait.

Top Spot
Big coalfish are frequently caught over the Plymouth wrecks by anglers targeting pollack.

Top Tip
Artificial eels, such as the Eddystone and Redgill patterns, work very well, both from the shore and boats.

Known in Scottish waters as the saithe, the coalfish is a member of the cod family, and it is often mistaken for, and bears a resemblance to, its cousin the pollack. The obvious difference between the two is that the lower jaw of the pollack protrudes the upper jaw and it has a barbule under the chin. The lateral line of the coalfish is different from that of the pollack as it is of light appearance on a dark background. Like other sea fishes, the coalfish will often vary in colour depending on what depth of water it is caught from. Shore-caught coalfish from relatively shallow water will appear very bright and silvery. They are often burnished with a tint of golden green and have a cream or white belly. Deep-water coalfish are more of a greeny-grey with pale, white bellies. They are very active hunters and form large shoals as they plunder small food fish. They will travel long distances in search of rich food supplies, such as herring fry and whitebait, and have been known to take small salmon smolts entering the sea in May.

Boat anglers tend to catch the bigger specimens over deep-water wrecks on a variety of baits. The smaller specimens come close into the shore and are more commonly caught from rocky shores during the hours of darkness.

Ling *(Molva molva)*

Current Records
Shore **21 lb 10 oz (9.809 kg)**
Boat **59 lb 8 oz (26.989 kg)**
World **82 lb (37.2 kg) Norway**

Season
All year round.

Distribution
Well distributed around the British coast but particularly off Cornwall. They are also common to the Orkneys, Shetland Isles and the west coast of Ireland. They can be found in the waters of the Arctic Circle, the coast of Iceland and Norway as well.

Natural Diet
Mostly small fish such as herring, flatfish, codling and pouting.

Top Spots
Wrecks off the north-east, south-west and Irish coasts. Ports such as Brixham in Devon and Bridlington in Yorkshire, are recognized for producing big ling hauls.

Top Tip
Try fishing over a wreck with a large baited pirk.

The largest and most prolific member of the cod family, the ling can reach a weight of 80 lb (36.3 kg) but is normally caught between 10–50 lb (4.54–22.68 kg). It is primarily a deep-water species living among the deep-water wrecks and reefs off the coast of Britain. Similar to an eel in shape, it can often extend to 6 ft (1.83 m) in length. Being a predator, it is well equipped to eat most smaller species and items of bait with its well-toothed mouth. As with the cod, the ling has a barbule hanging from the underside of the chin. Its long body is coated in slime secreted from the skin to form a protective covering against disease.

Coloration is normally of a greyish-brown marbled back with a creamy-white underside.

The ling is well distributed around the British coastline and favoured grounds lie off the south-west coast of Cornwall. Ling are mostly caught by boat anglers, but there are a few rocky, deep-water shore marks where ling to 20 lb (9.07 kg) have been caught by anglers fishing at night. They feed extensively on smaller species, and among the best baits are pouting and codling. For the novice angler out on a boat trip, ling can provide a good day's sport as they are relatively easy to catch. A large baited pirk is a good method to use for this species.

Flounder *(Platichthys flesus)*

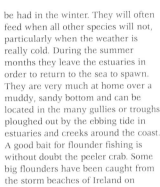

Current Records
Shore **5 lb 7 oz (2.466 kg)**
Boat **5 lb 11 oz 8 drm (2.594 kg)**

Season
All year round, but particularly in the winter.

Distribution
Common throughout the British Isles in creeks and estuaries.

Natural Diet
Crustaceans, worms, cockles and small crabs.

Top Spots
Rivers Teign, Plym, Yealm and Exe in south Devon, but also the River Tyne.

Top Tip
The addition of a flounder spoon about 6 in (15 cm) up the trace from the hook will help attract the flounder to your bait.

The flounder is a very popular species and is caught mainly from creeks or muddy estuaries. It is a member of the flatfish family and can be identified by the row of hard knobbly spots that trace the lateral line running from head to tail. Like the plaice, it has a splattering of orange spots, but the flounder is much darker in colour across the back. It has a large head and mouth, the skin texture along the back being smooth, apart from the knobbly bumps along the lateral line. The flounder can live quite happily in very brackish water and is often caught right at the top of the estuary where freshwater meets salt.

Not overlarge in size and mainly caught at between 2–3 lb (0.91–1.36 kg), the flounder can provide good sport on light tackle and is relatively easy to catch. It has a maximum size of around 6 lb (2.72 kg), and a 4 lb (1.81 kg) flounder is considered a specimen fish. It can be caught all year round, but the better sport is to be had in the winter. They will often feed when all other species will not, particularly when the weather is really cold. During the summer months they leave the estuaries in order to return to the sea to spawn. They are very much at home over a muddy, sandy bottom and can be located in the many gullies or troughs ploughed out by the ebbing tide in estuaries and creeks around the coast. A good bait for flounder fishing is without doubt the peeler crab. Some big flounders have been caught from the storm beaches of Ireland on peeler crab intended for bass.

Dab *(Pleuronectes limanda)*

Current Records
Shore **2 lb 9 oz 8 drm (1.177 kg)**
Boat **2 lb 12 oz 4 drm (1.248 kg)**

Season
March through to August.

Distribution
Present around the south-west coast of Britain in good numbers. Also spread widely along the European coastline.

Natural diet
Crabs, worms, fish fry, molluscs and several types of seaweed.

Top Spots
The Norfolk and Suffolk coastlines offer superb dab sport.

Top Tip
Because of the small mouth it is advisable to fish with small baits on small hooks. Many sea anglers use a short-shank, size 6 freshwater carp hook.

The smallest member of the flatfish family, the dab rarely exceeds 12 in (30 cm) in length. Sandy brown in colour, with a white creamy underside, it's very often mistaken for a small plaice by the beginner to sea angling. One quick way to spot the difference is to look at the lateral line on the top side of the dab. Trace the lateral line from behind the head at the opening to the gill cover, and you will see that it curves away slightly before becoming straight again. On the plaice it is straight, from the gill cover to the tail. Another way of telling the difference is to run your finger from tail to head on the back. You will find the skin is of a rough texture, while the same test on a plaice will reveal a smooth skin. At birth the dab is actually a round fish, and during growth the left eye moves around the head to take up position slightly forward of the right. The dab will then lie on its left side on the bottom of the sea bed with no impediment to its sight. When fishing sandy, open beaches, you are likely to encounter the dab. It is mainly found in shallow waters all around our coast and is also present in large numbers in inshore waters along the European coast all the way to Iceland.

Plaice (*Pleuronectes platessa*)

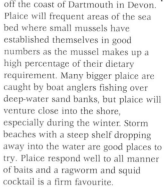

Current Records
Shore **8 lb 6 oz 14 drm (3.824 kg)**
Boat **10 lb 3 oz 8 drm (4.635 kg)**

Season
February through to end of September.

Distribution
All round the British coastline, they are very common in the deeper waters of the North Sea. They are also distributed as far north as Iceland and as far south as the Mediterranean.

Natural Diet
Mostly shellfish, such as razorfish, mussels and cockles. The strong mouth of the plaice is able to crush and grind away the shell to get to the inner meat. They also feed on most marine worms.

Top Spots
The Shambles Bank off Weymouth in Dorset is a well-known hot spot. Also Skerries Banks, south Devon.

Top Tip
The addition of half a dozen or so brightly coloured beads or sequins above the hook attracts plaice. Like other flatfish, they are very inquisitive.

The plaice is probably the best known member of the flatfish family, because of its easy identification. Colour will vary depending on the location and depth of water. However, it is usually marked with a dark brown back, with a series of orange or scarlet spots scattered at random over the skin. The eyes on the plaice, as with other flatfish, are positioned on the top side of the fish, allowing it to have a wide scope of vision while lying flat on the sea bed. The female plaice is capable of producing 250,000 eggs when spawning takes place early in the year in January or February.

Plaice do not grow to huge sizes, and a fish of 5 lb (2.27 kg) is considered a worthy specimen. Areas of the sea bed offering a sandy or shingle grit bottom are the ideal location for fishing. The most famous marks of all for plaice fishing are the Skerries Banks, a series of sand banks off the coast of Dartmouth in Devon. Plaice will frequent areas of the sea bed where small mussels have established themselves in good numbers as the mussel makes up a high percentage of their dietary requirement. Many bigger plaice are caught by boat anglers fishing over deep-water sand banks, but plaice will venture close into the shore, especially during the winter. Storm beaches with a steep shelf dropping away into the water are good places to try. Plaice respond well to all manner of baits and a ragworm and squid cocktail is a firm favourite.

Pollack (*Pollachius pollachius*)

Pollack are well documented as great sport-fish when hooked on light tackle. They have the ability to fight hard and often tear off on a heart-stopping run when first hooked. A member of the cod family, pollack are often confused with their close relative the coalfish. However, they can be easily recognized by the distinct protruding lower jaw. The jaw provides the fish with a means to disable its prey when attacking from below. Colouring is another form of identification when confusion arises between the two. The pollack is greenish-brown with a very dark lateral line, while the coalfish is more blue-black. The tail of the pollack is of a square appearance, whereas the coalfish has a defined fork in the centre of the tail fin. It is built with power and speed in mind, because as a predator, it has to move fast to ambush smaller species. The pollack can be located over rocky ground, but in the colder months bigger specimens stay well out in deeper water. Once the warmer weather arrives smaller pollack venture into the shallower water to feed, especially after the hours of darkness. They spawn early in the year, from March to the end of April.

Most shore-caught species rarely exceed 3 lb (1.36 kg), and to catch a bigger specimen you will have to hunt them out over deep-water wrecks. Pollack between 12–16 lb (5.44–7.26 kg) are plentiful from this type of area and can be caught on baited hooks or lures, such as artificial eels. For the beginner, the smaller pollack can offer great sport when fishing the night tide from a pier or harbour wall using float tackle.

Current Records
Shore **18 lb 4 oz (8.278 kg)**
Boat **29 lb 4 oz (13.268 kg)**

Season
Can be caught all year round, particularly in the south-west.

Distribution
Spread all around the coast of Britain especially off the south-west coast. Also present off the coast of Ireland and the Atlantic shores of Iceland.

Natural Diet
Small crabs, wrasse, sandeels, rocklings and prawns.

Top Spot
The Eddystone reef in Plymouth, Devon, is a prolific mark, as are most of the offshore wrecks along the south coast.

Top Tip
Using an artificial eel on light tackle over a wreck is the most exiting method for catching pollack. Drop the eel on a 15 ft (4.6 m) trace to the sea bed and wind up at a steady rate. If you feel the fish plucking at the eel don't stop, just keep on winding until it hooks itself.

Blue Shark *(Prionace glauca)*

Current Records
Shore **40 lb (18.14 kg)**
Boat **218 lb (98.88 kg)**
World **454 lb (205.93 kg) USA**

Season
May through to October.

Distribution
All around the British coastline and especially south-west Cornwall. They are also present around the southern and western shores of Ireland.

Natural Diet
Most smaller species of fish. The mackerel and herring are two prime examples.

Top Spot
South-west Cornish coast during the warmer months of the year.

Top Tip
When sharking, don't stop other activities such as mackerel fishing. The activity in the water will draw sharks closer to the boat.

A member of the shark family, the blue shark is one of the two most common around UK coastlines, the other being the porbeagle. Blue sharks can be found in the warmer waters of the southern coast of Britain, especially around the Cornish coastline. It takes its name from its distinctive dark-blue back and light-blue flanks. However, once removed from the sea and killed, its blue coat fades away to a dreary grey colour. The blue shark is a voracious predator and has been known to attack swimmers off beaches.

It can grow to over 12 ft (3.66 m) in length, and blue sharks over 200 lb (90.72 kg) have been caught in British waters. Evidence suggests they can grow much larger, but smaller fish in the 60–70 lb (21–31.75 kg) class are more commonly caught. A fish of this size can be a very testing target for the novice fisherman.

Like other species of shark, the blue has what is known as a spiracle or an opening behind the eye. This is connected to the gill system, which controls respiration. They have no swim bladder and regulate their buoyancy by controlling the amount of water within the body cavity.

The blue shark is a roving species and can be found in deep-water areas off rocky, cliff-lined shores. Where there is a good supply of smaller prey fish the blue shark will not be far away. In the warmer weather they will venture close to the shore in pursuit of food.

Thornback Ray *(Raja clavata)*

Probably the most widely caught member of the ray family, thornbacks are so named because of the array of thorny spines that adorn the tail and wings. The mouth is positioned on the underside, allowing it to move over the sea bed and cover its selected food item before passing it through a set of grinding teeth, which are powerful enough to crush shells and molluscs. The eyes are set on the top side, and it is thought that eyesight is very poor; instead the thornback relies on an internal radar system, thought to be triggered by a form of electromagnetism and vibration. Directly behind the eyes are two holes which are breathing vents or spiracles. Coloration of the body varies depending on the type of bottom the ray is living over. The adult thornback is usually a pale brownish-yellow and is coated in patchy black speckles. Towards the rear of the body and

extending down the tail there will often be a brownish-red pigment to the skin. Thornback rays are not commonly found in very deep water, preferring the inshore clean grounds of sand and mud. They are a popular target for both dinghy and shore anglers, who are advised to take time when striking at a thornback bite, in order for the ray to work the bait well into its mouth. They are not caught in huge sizes and are the second smallest species in the ray family. A specimen of 15 lb (6.8 kg) is a good catch, and thornbacks above this weight tend to be females. They are often found close to estuaries and even travel up into the estuary to feed on sandeels.

Current Records
Shore **21 lb 12 oz (9.866 kg)**
Boat **31 lb 7 oz (14.26 kg)**

Season
March through to the end of October.

Distribution
Throughout the British Isles, Ireland, North Sea, Baltic Sea and the Mediterranean Sea.

Natural Diet
Being a predator, it thrives on small fish such as young flatfish, sandeels, herrings, sprats and crustaceans.

Top Spots
The Thames Estuary and Bristol Channel are famous for their thornback ray fishing.

Top Tip
Early on in the season the top bait is a chunk of fresh herring. As the summer approaches, fresh peeler crabs take over as the number one bait. On the east coast, hermit crabs are another favoured bait.

Common Skate *(Raja batis)*

The common skate belongs to the skate family, three of whose members are of importance to the sea angler: the white skate, the long-nosed skate and the common skate.

The common skate is sometimes referred to as the blue or grey skate, from its greyish-blue coloration when first taken from the sea. They are usually a dark, greenish-brown colour across the top side, with a whitish-grey underside littered with dark-rimmed pores, and will often have golden-coloured spots and pinkish stripes on the back. The body is shaped like a diamond, while the front end resembles the head of a shovel. Like other skates and rays they have two large holes, spiracles, just behind the eyes. Skates breathe through these for if, like other species, they had to take water in through their mouths, they would not survive, as each breath would mean a mouthful of mud.

Once common around the whole coast of Britain, these giants of the sea are mainly sought after off the Western Isles of Scotland. They grow to a huge size, up to 8 ft (2.44 m) in length, live in waters of up to 600 ft (183 m) deep and have been caught weighing 150 lb (68 kg) or more. Many anglers who fish for skate return their quarry to the sea after capture in a bid to preserve this wonderful creature. The larger common skate can be found over sand and mud bottoms and spends much of its time half-buried in the sea bed. This gives it the cover to seize its prey. Smaller common skate are often found in shallower water.

Thick-lipped Mullet *(Chelon labrosus)*

There are three species of grey mullet that the angler is likely to observe while out fishing: the golden grey, the thin-lipped and the most common, the thick-lipped. When they are small they are often confused with the bass, but there are a few differences that help to identify them correctly. Mullet have large scales all over the body, even over their gill covers, unlike the bass. It is possible to tell the age of a good-sized mullet from the scales by counting the number of rings present. The thick-lipped mullet is coloured in a shade of grey across the back and has a white belly. As the name suggests, it has a pair of thick lips, and contrary to belief can be hooked and caught by the angler. Mullet have long been surrounded by a myth that they are uncatchable, and if hooked by the angler they are easily lost, because of their soft lips. However, although they are a shy, clever fish and often seem to ignore anglers' baits, they can be caught, and the lips of the mullet are actually quite tough.

Thick-lipped mullet move in shoals and feed close to the surface on small crustaceans and vegetable matter. They have poor teeth, so food is swallowed and broken down in the stomach. They can be located close to the shore and in summer are present in many harbours and estuaries. Visit any harbour in the warmer months and you will see the mullet cruising around just under the surface, searching out scraps of food and sucking items of waste from the underside of fishing boats. As they are able to tolerate brackish water, they are very often caught in the lower reaches and estuaries of many river systems.

Mackerel *(Scomber scombrus)*

The mackerel is one of the hardest fighting sea species. Similar in looks to its relative the tuna fish, mackerel are built for speed and power. The head is pointed, and the sleek, slim body resembles a torpedo, finishing off with a large, forked tail. It has a very distinctive coloration with a metallic, marine blue back, shaded over with black bars. When the fish is removed from water the colour soon fades away to a dull grey. The white flanks and underside of the species are covered with a film of silver, pink, gold and blue, which shines like a rainbow.

The mackerel spends its time in search of fry and sandeels. They will charge headlong into a shoal of fry, twisting and turning at speed with mouths open until they catch their prey.

Mackerel are often caught on feathers or by float fishing. Being a shoal fish, mackerel can be caught in great numbers. It is thought that the mackerel never stops swimming, and as they are always on the move, more water passes through the gills, helping them to breathe more easily while maintaining fast, active movement. Spawning in the months of January through to June, they are a slow-growing species and it is thought that a mackerel of 1 lb (0.45 kg) in weight could be as old as eight years. During the winter they head for the deeper, warmer waters of the Irish Sea, while in the spring they move back into the shallow waters. Huge shoals can often be seen breaking the surface as they chase brit or sandeels in summer.

Current Records
Shore **5 lb 11 oz 14 drm (2.605 kg)**
Boat **6 lb 2 oz 7 drm (2.791 kg)**

Season
April to October, with the peak season for the shore angler in June and July.

Distribution
Present in large numbers around the coastline of Cornwall. Other hot spots include the North Yorkshire coastline, the south of Ireland and west Scotland.

Natural Diet
Plankton, squid, brit, whitebait, sandeels and any small fry.

Top Spots
Most piers and breakwater walls around the UK. Rock marks such as Hope's Nose and Berry Head in south Devon are well-known mackerel marks.

Top Tip
When fishing with float tackle, fish the bait very shallow, set at a depth of 4 ft (1.22 m) or even less. Mackerel spend a lot of time near the surface chasing smaller fry.

Turbot *(Scopthalmus maximus)*

The turbot is one of the most prized members of the flatfish family and makes an excellent meal for the angler's table. It is similar to the brill, both in looks and habits. Identification in comparison to the brill can be made from the shape of the body, as turbot are round. Another form of identification is the number of rays featured on the anal fin. The turbot has around 46, while the brill is blessed with some 60, housed on a longer fin. Turbot are coloured to blend in with their surroundings and are usually of a light brown or sandy appearance on the top with a spattering of fine, bony tubercles.

They bear a resemblance to a polished marble surface and are masters of disguise when half-buried in the sandy bottom of the sea bed. The large mouth can accommodate a whole small fish when the jaws are fully extended. It is fitted with very fine teeth running up each side to grip the food. Turbot spawn in the months of March to June, and a female is capable of laying 10 million eggs, each one being 1 mm in size.

Turbot can be found in good numbers around the coast of Britain and enjoy the rich hunting grounds of sandy bays and the sides of shallow, sloping sandbanks. They are also caught close to estuary marks that have muddy bottoms and many of the deep-water wrecks. Capable of growing upwards of 30 lb (13.61 kg) in weight, they can give the sea angler a good spirited fight if they are hooked on light tackle. They can often be caught by drifting a moving bottom bait over the slopes of a sandbank once the tide starts to run. The turbot will follow a moving bait for some distance before moving in and attacking the bait.

Current Records
Shore **28 lb 8 oz (12.927 kg)**
Boat **33 lb 12 oz (15.3 kg)**

Season
From May through to the end of October.

Distribution
Widespread around the coast of Britain, but more so in the south-west.

Natural Diet
Shrimps, sandeels, sprats, whiting and small flatfish.

Top Spots
Around the offshore wrecks off the north-east coast and the Shambles Bank off Weymouth, Dorset.

Top Tip
Use a long trace of around 8–12 ft (2.44–3.66 m), baited with sandeel or mackerel strip.

Lesser-spotted Dogfish *(Scyllium canicula)*

The lesser-spotted dogfish is the most common of the dogfish to be found around the British coast. It is a member of the shark family, and although it bears a similarity in looks, it is considerably smaller. Often called the roughhound because of its sandpaper-textured skin, it can be easily identified by the newcomer to sea angling by the vast array of spots peppered over its back and sides. Its orange-brown back and pale cream belly distinguish the lesser-spotted dogfish from its close cousin the greater-spotted dogfish. The greater-spotted has larger spots, and the two have different positioning of the nose flaps. On the greater-spotted dogfish the nose flap does not join and is positioned above the mouth, while on

the lesser-spotted dogfish the nose flap is continuous and almost joins the mouth. Their eyesight is poor, and the dogfish relies on its keen sense of smell to hunt down prey. Its small sharp teeth are used to bite and tear at food.

Caught from both boat and shore, the lesser-spotted dogfish can be located over sandy, muddy or gravel bottom areas. When caught, the angler may experience difficulty in holding the fish still, and the dogfish may inflict a nasty graze with its rough skin. The correct way to immobilize the fish is to hold the dogfish behind the head, bringing the tail up to meet it. It has a skeleton of cartilage rather than hard bone and held in this way you will do no harm to the fish.

Current Records
Shore **4 lb 15 oz 3 drm (2.245 kg)**
Boat **4 lb 6 oz 8 drm (1.998 kg)**

Season
April through to November.

Distribution
Widespread throughout the British Isles, North Sea and Mediterranean Sea.

Natural Diet
Crabs, lobsters, shrimps, prawns, sandeels and small flatfish.

Top Spot
The Welsh coast offers some superb dogfish sport, both from shore and boat. Pick a sandy beach fringed by rocks.

Top Tip
A three-hook paternoster rig with size 2/0 sea hooks baited with either mackerel or sandeel is the top method for catching good dogfish.

Dover Sole *(Solea solea)*

A member of the flatfish family, the name Dover derives from the days when the sole was transported from the Kent coast to the London restaurants for the gentry to eat. Sometimes called slips or tongues because of their small size and resemblance to an animal's tongue, the Dover sole is of a pale brown colour with darker patches and widespread speckling across its top side. It does not grow to a large size, and a sole of 2 lb (0.91 kg) is regarded as a fine specimen. Like others in the flatfish family, the eyes are mounted close together on the right or upper side of the body. The underside or belly is pure white, although on some occasions colouring does occur over the belly on freak fish. For quick identification, there is a dark spot located on the tip of the right pectoral fin. It has a small mouth, which explains why not many are caught by anglers who normally use big baits. The entire body, with the exception of the underside of the head, is coated in tiny scales, giving the Dover sole a rough texture to its skin while its

cousin the lemon sole is smooth to touch and has bigger blotches on the back. When caught commercially and presented at the table, the skin is removed by peeling it from the body in one continuous strip.

Spawning usually takes place between the months of March and May over inshore marks in warmer water. When the colder weather arrives the sole moves back out to deeper water, and in extremely low temperatures becomes almost comatose. Dover sole like gravel and sandy sea beds, burying themselves under the surface of the sand to make themselves less conspicuous to predators. Anglers in search of the Dover sole should fish with small hooks and very small pieces of ragworm or lugworm bait.

Current Records
Shore **6 lb 8 oz 10 drm (2.966 kg)**
Boat **4 lb 1 oz 12 drm (1.864 kg)**

Season
April through to the end of September.

Distribution
Spread throughout the English Channel, west coast of Ireland and the Irish Sea, scarcer in the north of Scotland.

Natural Diet
Crustaceans, molluscs, sandeels, worms and small fishes.

Top Spot
The town beach at Aldeburgh in Suffolk is a well-known sole hot spot.

Top Tip
Let bites develop: sole have small mouths, and it takes time for them to reach the hook, even with small bait.

Black Bream *(Spondyliosoma cantharus)*

Current Records
Shore **5 lb 2 drm (2.272 kg)**
Boat **6 lb 14 oz 4 drm (3.126 kg)**

Season
May through to September.

Distribution
Found in coastal waters all around the British Isles and Channel Islands.

Natural Diet
Small blennies, crustaceans, marine worms, plankton and seaweed.

Top Spots
The south coast ports; Littlehampton, Hayling, Lymington and Poole.

Top Tip
A ragworm tipped with a strip of squid.

The black bream shares many of the characteristics of the marine fish family Sparidae. Its colouring and shape give a clue to its name, as its deep-bodied shape is similar to that of the freshwater bream. Colouring on the black bream may vary slightly, depending on the area and the depth of water from which it is caught. The flanks are normally grey or silver, with the back dark grey with a blue sheen, shading into black around the top of the back.

This fully scaled species has a long dorsal fin with sharp spines and a shorter anal fin fitted with three further spines. It has a small head in comparison with the body and the

upper jaw is fitted with a front row of sharp white teeth. Sitting behind these are an additional set of curved, needle-like teeth. The black bream spawns in April or May and differs from other sea bream as it makes a nest on the bottom of the sea bed to lay its spawn in.

In recent years the black bream has not been caught in the large numbers previously seen. This has been attributed to overfishing. However, stocks are said to be on the increase off the south coast of Britain.

Black bream do not grow to a great size, and a bream of 3 lb (1.36 kg) can be considered a fine specimen of a fish. They are more commonly caught by boat anglers fishing over areas of broken rocky ground and reefs. Some of the smaller fish do get caught from the shore, but this tends to be from marks in deeper water. A broken reef with a wreck located on it is the ideal hunting ground for the black bream. Here it can feed in the safety of deep water on small crustaceans, plankton and seaweed. Black bream are renowned as a sporty, hard fighter on appropriate tackle.

Spurdog *(Squalus acanthias)*

A member of the shark family, the spurdog is easily distinguished from other dogfish. There are two main features that determine the species, one of which is the two extremely sharp spines present on the back, at the front of each of the two dorsal fins. To the unwary angler these spines can inflict a nasty cut that may require medical attention. When handling, the spurdog should be held by the neck of the tail with one hand and supported by the underside of the throat with the other. This will stop the spurdog from twisting its tail around the arm or wrist of the angler. The other aid to identification is the absence of the anal fin present on other members of the dogfish group. Looking very much like a small shark, it lacks the third eyelid or membrane, used to cover or clean the eyeball, present in the shark family group. Spur-dogs are also sometimes mistaken

for tope by the novice angler. The spurdog has a dreary, pale, greyish back and sides, with a pale white underside. The long and slender body is built for speed, and it travels in packs when hunting prey, usually at a mid-water depth. The mouth contains a set of sharp teeth built for ripping and shredding prey fish.

It is more likely to be caught from the boat by the angler fishing for other species. This is due to the fact that the spurdog prefers the deeper water marks of clean sandy bottoms. However, a few are caught from the shore, and the bulk of these have been identified as females, probably because the female of the species moves into shallower waters to expel her young during the months of August and October.

Current Records
Shore **16 lb 12 oz 8 drm ((7.612 kg)**
Boat **21 lb 3 oz 7 drm (9.623 kg)**

Season
May through to November, sometimes late December.

Distribution
Present throughout the British Isles, they are caught in larger numbers from the western coast.

Natural Diet
Any small fish, including soles, sprats, sardines, squids and sandeels.

Top Spots
Boats out of Swansea and Rhyl, Wales, catch lots of spurdogs. Scottish sea lochs are also renowned for their spurdog sport.

Top Tip
Herring are one of the top spurdog baits. In some areas a large chunk of garfish flesh is favoured.

Natural Baits

The sea angler has a wealth of baits at his or her disposal and is blessed with many free offerings from the sea shore. From ragworm to razorfish, a good angler will never be short of the right bait for the species sought. Modern-day tackle shops offer a wide variety of commercially produced blast-frozen baits, which will be totally fresh. The bigger shops, in particular, will have a good weekly trade in freshly dug live worms and regular supplies of the much-prized peeler crab. You can also buy fresh sea baits straight from the fish markets as the daily catch is landed. Even the local fishmonger's shop might have what you are looking for. Bait often plays second fiddle to quality tackle, but a fresh bait in educated hands will out-fish an expensive fishing rod and poor quality bait. There is no excuse for presenting a poor quality bait, especially if you are able to collect or dig your own. If you are lucky enough to be in a position to do this, and you can combine quality bait with good angling skills, the rewards can be high.

Peeler Crab

This is probably the most popular bait used by the sea angler, and it is used up and down the coast as it attracts a variety of different species. It gets its name from the fact that it sheds or peels its skin at several stages throughout its life.

When the crab is in a state of peeling it is a much sought-after bait. Due to the sheer demand, the price of peeler crabs in tackle shops can soar in the winter months, when they are in very short supply. If you are lucky enough to live near an estuary where peelers are present, you may be in a position to collect them yourself at low tide. Many anglers have established areas of the sea shore where they have placed special peeler traps. These usually consist of a length of broken pipe or a semi-circular roof tile, which the crab will hide under while peeling its shell. The trap is inserted into the mud or shingle at an angle, allowing the peeler to crawl under it to shed its shell. When the tide drops the crab will be found sheltering deep in the back end of the trap. It's hard work collecting peelers, and in some areas you may only find five crabs in 100 traps per tide. However, if you are fishing in competitions in the winter, it's well worth the effort, for this is without doubt a superior bait.

Peeler crabs are widely used for flounder and cod fishing and are easy to prepare for the hook. If you look at the shell on the back of the crab you will see a split forming around the base of the shell near to the legs. With your thumb and forefinger gently prise the shell upwards and it will come off. This will reveal a soft skin and once exposed it is a deadly bait.

To make the bait go further the crab can be cut into two sections. Simply take a knife and cut down through the centre of the body. Don't discard the legs as they are a good bait in their own right. The legs, once peeled, can either be used to hold the body of the crab on the hook, or can be used by themselves as a bait. By picking away the shell at the end of the legs you will soon be able to peel away the rest of the protective coating to reveal the soft flesh.

The best way to store peelers is to collect them and keep them alive in a bucket, covering them with damp seaweed. If you are going to keep

TOP: Peeler crabs are regarded by many sea anglers as the top bait for a large variety of species.

LEFT: Search around the sea shore as the tide drops away and a wealth of free bait becomes available.

them for a few days you will need to replace the seaweed as it will dry out. It is advisable to remove any dead or dying peelers from the bucket and freeze them, but peel them first before freezing. They should be frozen individually and wrapped in clear (plastic) film to protect them from freezer burn. Before freezing, remove the gills, which can be found at the side of the crab under the eyes. This will help to keep them fresher if they are to be frozen for a long period.

Hooking Peeler Crab

To get the best from your bait it is advisable to peel the body completely and remove the gills and legs. The legs should also be fully peeled. Lay the peeled crab on its back and cut the body in half long-ways, down through the centre with a knife. Take

half the body and thread the point of the hook through the leg sockets, starting at one end and working up through the sockets to the other. The crab should be quite secure on the hook at this stage.

To enhance the bait and help to keep the body on the hook if casting a fair distance, the legs can be impaled on the hook below the body. Using the legs in this manner will give the impression of the bait being a whole, live crab. If you like to fish at a long distance and place a considerable force on the bait when casting, use an elastic cotton thread to bind the bait into position on the hook for added security.

RIGHT: Quite often anglers will use crab mixed with another type of bait to form a cocktail. Here it is being used with lugworm.

Mounting a Peeler Crab

1 Peeler crab has long been regarded as a top all-round sea-angling bait. It is widely used in competitions and is attractive to all manner of species.

2 Fresh crabs should be used when they are ready to shed their shells and are completely peeled as shown, including the legs.

3 Take a sharp knife and cut the body of the crab almost in half. Leave a hinge in the flesh at the lower end of the crab like this.

4 Start to thread the crab on to the hook. For shore fishing this should be a size 1/0 or 2/0. Thread the hook in and out of the leg sockets, to hold the crab in position on the hook.

5 Once the crab has been mounted, if you are casting long distances, hold the crab in place by winding elasticated cotton around the body as shown above.

6 To complement the body part of the crab, the legs should now be added to the hook. This is called "tipping a bait" and gives the appearance of a whole, live crab.

Mackerel

Mackerel is widely available to the angler and is a top sea bait for a variety of species. They can be caught on feathers, purchased frozen from the tackle shop, or bought fresh from the fishmonger's shop.

There are many methods of presenting mackerel on the hook, as it can be used in its whole form or cut into small strips. Most shore anglers cut fillets, one from each side, and then cut these into small strips. To cut the fillets away from the bone, simply hold the mackerel down on a cutting board by the head and insert a sharp knife into the flesh behind the gills. Cut so that the knife blade reaches the central bone. Then turn the knife away from the head, cutting all the way down the body to the tail. By keeping the knife blade flat and following the top of the central bone, the knife will exit at the wrist of the tail. The cut fillet should lift away from the main body in one piece.

If you then require a number of smaller strips of mackerel flesh it is simply a case of cutting uniform strips from one of the fillets. When you are shore fishing with float tackle for mackerel and garfish it is advisable to cut small strips.

Boat anglers fishing for conger eels, tope or sharks will use what is known as a "flapper". This is a whole mackerel with the backbone cut away to leave the head and side fillets intact. When presented on the hook, the fillets flap around in the tide, giving the impression the bait is on the move. If you catch a few mackerel next time you are out fishing, why not gut and freeze them to use later on in the year. If you are freezing mackerel it is a good idea to wrap them individually in clear film (plastic wrap) after cleaning them, as this will protect the flesh from freezer burn.

Hooking Mackerel

For boat fishing, anglers will usually use a whole or half-mackerel bait, depending on the species they are fishing for. For larger species, such as conger, a whole mackerel is the standard approach. The mackerel is mounted up whole on a large hook in a fashion known as a "flapper bait". This consists of a whole mackerel that has had the backbone removed, giving the appearance of a moving target for the conger to grab at. This also helps

1 Whole mackerel are a good bottom fishing bait for conger eels. They can be prepared for the hook as follows and should be fished on a large hook and a wire trace.

2 Take a sharp knife and cut the mackerel in half from the gill cover near the head to the tail end. Make sure you keep the knife flat against the central backbone.

3 Turn the mackerel over and repeat the process until you have two cut wings as shown. Now remove the backbone so you have just the head of the mackerel and the two side fillets.

to release a very strong scent trail for the fish to home in on. The seahook, which should be a size 6/0 or 8/0, is passed through the head with the point left clear.

When fishing for bass or cod a simple whole side fillet can be mounted on the hook by passing the hook through the bait at the top of the fillet twice. This will ensure the bait stays firmly on the hook, but it allows the tail end of the fillet to move freely in the tide, imitating a small fish.

The shore angler will be using smaller baits for species like garfish, cod, dogfish, whiting and even mackerel themselves. The most common way of preparing a shore bait when using mackerel is to cut it into long strips. Each strip is then used as an individual bait on a small seahook, such as a 1/0. When cutting the strips it is a good idea to make the cuts at an angle across the body so the bottom of the strip tapers down to a point. The hook is inserted through the top end of the strip once only. Once presented in the water the strip of mackerel will give the appearance of a small fish or fry; this is perfect for any larger fish on the lookout for a free meal.

4 These are the two methods of presenting a mackerel "flapper bait". Use a large hook and wire trace with both because, when fished on the bottom, a large fish such as a conger eel is expected to take the bait.

5 The most widely way of preparing mackerel for shore fishing is to cut it into strips. Cut at an angle with the strips tapering downwards. This is a good bait for cod, dogfish and whiting.

RIGHT: Buy fillets of mackerel for shore fishing. Let them thaw and then prepare them as shown above.

OPPOSITE: Fresh mackerel can be caught on feathers, either cooked to eat or used as a bait.

ABOVE: Frozen mackerel can be bought from your local tackle shop in packs of two or more. It is a good idea to buy whole mackerel if you are fishing for large species such as congers, dogfish or cod, or if you are boat fishing and cannot catch fresh mackerel bait. Make sure the mackerel is straight as it will be easier to prepare.

Lugworms

The yellowtail lugworm is highly favoured by sea anglers as it is a natural bait. The name yellowtail derives from the fact that once handled, the worm emits a yellow iodine liquid, which will stain the angler's hand. The black lugworm is so named because of its black colouring caused by the black mud it passes through its body when digging its burrow. It can be dug from muddy shore lines as the tide recedes. Some of the best yellowtail lug comes from the shore around Kent. It can be purchased from tackle shops or anglers can dig their own. To dig your own you will need a fork or a device known as a bait pump. You will also need a collection bucket or a container to keep the worms in while digging for others. Digging with a fork can be hard work and may take a considerable amount of time to collect a hundred or so worms.

A bait pump is a type of pump-action tube inserted into the mud over what is known as the worm cast. The worm is sucked into the chamber of the pump when suction is applied by lifting the handle. To operate the pump you will first need to find a worm cast, which is a mark left by the worm where it has come to the surface and begun to burrow back down again.

Place the pump over the cast and push it slightly into the ground. When you have the pump set in the ground, pull up the handle and this will create a vacuum, which traps the mud and worm in the cylinder of the pump. Once the pump has been withdrawn the handle is pushed down, spewing the contents out on to the floor. You then pick up any worms caught in the pump and place them in your bucket.

There are also specialist lugworm spades available from good tackle shops. These are a worthwhile investment if the worms you seek are in deep burrows, sometimes as deep as 2 ft (60 cm) below the surface. To store the lugworms it is preferable to use a shallow tray with a small amount of sea water in the bottom. The tray should be kept in the bottom of a fridge to keep it at an even, cool temperature, and the sea water should be changed each day. Any dead or dying worms should be removed. You can freeze lugworms by first squeezing out their innards, and then

TOP: **Black lugworms are widely used for cod fishing and should be threaded on the hook like this.**

ABOVE CENTRE: **Common or blow lugworms can be dug from the beach.**

ABOVE: **Lugworms can be dug with a fork, or a special bait pump can be used.**

wrapping them individually in newspaper. Frozen in this manner they will keep for long periods. When defrosted, this tough, rubbery worm is a good bait for winter cod fishing.

Common Lugworms

Common lugworms, or blow lugworms as they are often called, are more usually found in a sandy environment. They can be dug from many beaches around the coastline. They can also be found in estuaries and make an excellent bait for many different species, including cod and whiting. As with the yellowtail lugworm, their burrow holes can be identified by the cast they leave on the surface of the sand. Unlike the yellowtail, the common lug favours a U-shaped tunnel or burrow, which rarely exceeds 15 in (38 cm). When spotting the cast on the surface it is advisable to look for the blow hole, which will be a short way behind the cast. This will give you a rough idea of where the worm will be lying before you attempt to dig down to it.

For collection purposes, a bucket and garden fork will be needed. During the warmer months the worms can be dug out of the sand or mud with a fork quite easily. However, in colder weather they will burrow slightly deeper and will be harder to find. To store them, simply collect them in a bucket containing a small amount of sea water. If you are going to keep them for a couple of days, store them in a fridge in a shallow tray with a shallow covering of sea water. Using this method it is possible to keep them alive for a considerable amount of time. Common lugworms do not make good baits for freezing, the problem being that the content of the common lugworm is mainly water.

Hooking Lugworms

When fishing for cod and casting lugworms any distance it is advisable to get as many as five or six worms on the same hook. It will help if the hook is of the long shank variety. To hook them, simply enter the hook point into the centre of the head and thread the hook right down through the centre of the body. Once on the hook, the worm is worked up the long shank and over the eye. Keep doing this until you have enough worms on the hook. It's usually the

Hooking Sandeels

When fishing for bass in a tidal run it is better to present the eel on a long trace with minimal or no weight. A single split shot can be used to force the eel down in the water, leaving it to swim freely. If you need more weight due to the pull of the tide, a small drilled ball weight can be used free-running on the line. When hooking sandeels for this method it is important that they are only lightly hooked so they can swim unhindered. A size 1 or even size 2 Aberdeen-style hook should be inserted into the flesh under the jaw once only. To fish a frozen eel in the same manner as described above it is advisable to pass the hook through the mouth and exit it just behind the gills. The hook will act as a means of support in keeping the eel upright and will let the tail sway in the flow in a natural manner. For other species, like rays, the hook is passed all the way through the eel's body. The point of the hook is then left pointing out from the side of the eel near the tail. This is done because a ray will often take a moment or two to take the bait well into its mouth. Approaching the eel from behind, the hook is therefore in the right position to enable a good hook hold should the ray try and eject the bait. Sandeels can be cut in half when used fresh or frozen, and fished under a float for pollack, mackerel and garfish.

case that the tail of the last worm is left hanging from the hook in an enticing manner. It's important to fill the hook completely if you are casting any distance, because live lugworms are a very soft bait and the impact on the worms when casting may result in some being lost while the tackle is in flight. When hooking frozen black lugworm you can be sure they will stay on the hook because of their thick, rubbery skin. A tip that many sea anglers use is to inject the skin with a flavour or oil before casting. This replaces the innards removed before freezing.

Sandeels

Sandeels are a terrific all-round sea bait and can be used alive or frozen. If you live in the south-west of Britain you may have seen them caught in large seine nets from the local beaches. It is best to get live sandeels, and species such as bass, pollack and rays are suckers for them. Once purchased or caught they can be stored for long periods in a floating wooden box known as a courge. The courge can be kept in sea water and tied to a mooring buoy until you need the eels. The sides of the box have very small holes to allow a constant flow of sea water to enter and leave, thus keeping the sandeels alive. If fishing from boat or shore you will need a bucket with an aerator pump to keep the eels in tip-top condition. Used alive, the sandeel is rated highly as a bass bait.

A small hook is used so as not to damage the eel or unbalance it. The hook is pushed through the skin under the jaw, and the eel is left to

swim freely. It is advisable to use little or no weight on the line, and many bass specialists use a single split shot weight to take the eel down in the tide. If you can't get hold of live sandeels then the next best thing is a packet of good quality frozen ones. Many bait companies use a blast-freezing process, which keeps the sandeel as fresh as the day it was caught. Frozen sandeels can be presented whole, cut into halves or used in strips. In the summer they can often be dug from the sand right on the tide line as the water drops. You will need a fork to do this and a quick eye to spot the eels as they try to burrow away in the soft sand.

TOP: Lugworm being threaded on to a Pennell rig. This is a good bait to use in a cocktail with crab or squid.

RIGHT: Sandeels can usually be bought from the local tackle dealer and are available live and frozen. Live sandeels are best if you can get them.

BELOW: The best form of presentation using a live sandeel is to mount it on a single hook. The sandeel then moves naturally in the water. They are a good bait for bass.

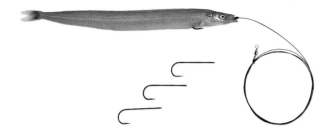

Razorfish

The razorfish is an excellent bait and is widely used for bass, cod and flatfish. It takes its name from the razor-shaped shell that surrounds the body. There are four species of razorfish found in British waters, and the most common is the pod razor which is usually about 3–5 in (7.62–12.7 cm) in length.

Razors can be gathered from the beach after a storm and are usually found right on the tide line buried beneath the sand. Anglers who have collected razors will be aware of a neat little trick you can employ to get the razor up to the surface of the sand. Take a bag of household salt, sprinkle it down the keyhole-shaped depressions in the sand, which are the razor's burrows. After a short time they will come up to the surface and investigate the irritating salt, thus giving away their presence. When spotted they should be held tightly until they relinquish their grip. Try and keep movement and sound to a bare minimum because once the razorfish are aware of your presence, they will bury deeper into the sand. You may need to use a fork to dig them out, and this is hard work as they move down through the sand very quickly. To prise the meat out, insert a knife carefully into the hinge of the shell. Don't force the shell apart as all this will do is tear the meat inside. The main attraction as a bait is

ABOVE: Razors come in all shapes and sizes and can be frozen. Fresh razorfish can be dug from the sand on a storm beach and should be kept stored in sea water. The orange-and-cream meat inside the razor is a particularly good bass bait.

BELOW: Many anglers buy frozen calamari squid in bulk packs like this.

the meaty foot, which, when placed on a hook, will support the rest of the body. Razors are best used fresh when the meat is tough. After freezing, the meat tends to go soft and it becomes difficult to keep on the hook. If you have enough razors and wish to freeze them, it is advisable to blanch them in the shell with boiling water before freezing. This will help to make the skin tougher. However, as with many other baits, there is no substitute for a fresh razor, which is a great bait for bass and cod in the winter.

Hooking Razorfish

For best results, small razors can be hooked in a similar fashion to worm baits. This will involve taking the whole razor from the shell and threading the hook down through the centre of the flesh. As they are only 3 in (7.5 cm) long it is advisable to present two on the hook. Bigger razors can be used as a single bait and are threaded on in the same manner. The tough, fleshy skin of the foot can be used to keep the bait on the hook once the main body has been threaded on. Razors cut into smaller bits are good for tipping lugworm baits when cod fishing. The tough texture of the skin helps keep the softer worm on the hook.

Squid

Squid is a widely used sea fishing bait and is probably more readily available than any other bait in Britain. Both the large common squid caught by commercial fishermen in the North Sea and the calamari squid, which is smaller in size and imported, are available to the angler in most tackle shops or fishmongers. Commercially caught squid is bigger and is cream in skin colour with yellowy white flesh. Calamari is smaller, 6–7 in (15–20 cm) long, but has a similar colouring. Squid is a very versatile sea bait and can be used on its own or mixed with other baits on the hook to provide a cocktail bait. Frozen squid bought from the tackle shop is usually of the calamari type and when defrosted can be used in two ways. When boat fishing for bass, cod or congers over deep-water marks the squid can be used as a whole bait. As the bait bounces across the bottom it looks almost alive and is eagerly taken by bigger species. Shore anglers tend to remove the plastic-type backbone found in the squid and cut them into long strips. These strips can be threaded up the hook to the eye and are long enough to leave a trailing tail, so simulating a worm bait. This is a great method for black and red bream.

ABOVE: The most popular type of squid is the calamari, which is approximately 6 in (15 cm) in length. Whole calamari squid is a good bait for larger fish such as bass and cod.

Hooking Squid

For bigger species, such as bass and cod, a whole calamari squid mounted up on a double-hook Pennell rig is the best method. The squid can be mounted in such a way that it seems alive. If using a single hook with a whole calamari, it is advisable to bind the body section to the line above the eye of the hook. This will stop it slipping down on to the shank of the hook. Bigger common squid can be cleaned and gutted. In the centre of a

Preparing Squid

1 Spread the squid on a board and allow it to thaw. Squid can be either used whole for large fish or cut into strips for smaller species.

3 Once the head has been removed, cut open the body and remove the plastic-type backbone, the ink sac and all the innards.

squid you will find the ink bag used for squirting its enemies, while running up the back you will find a transparent, plastic-type quill. This is removed, and the skin is peeled off to reveal the white flesh. The squid's body is then slit open using a sharp knife. Once opened out, it can be cut into whatever size strips of flesh you require. For bigger species use bigger strips and for smaller species, such as bream and whiting, use the squid in small, fine strips.

2 If you plan to use the squid in strips the first thing to do is to remove the head. Do this with a sharp knife as shown.

4 The cape or body can then be cut into small strips and used for smaller species, or the squid can be mounted whole as shown.

Cockles

Easy to collect from the sea shore, the cockle is a great bait for catching dabs and other flatfish. Cockles can be gathered in their hundreds on the sea shore at low tide, and shingle banks and estuaries are popular places to look for them. To collect them you will need a garden rake and a sack to put them in. By raking back the surface of the shore, cockles can be found lying in abundance.

ABOVE: Cockles can be gathered from the sea shore and are a good bait for all forms of flatfish.

BELOW: Being a small bait, cockles are used two or three at a time to make sure the hook is covered.

Cockles are best prepared by being immersed in boiling water for a few seconds. The shell is prised open with using a pointed instrument such as a knife. If you want to keep a good supply on the go, tie a sack to a mooring buoy, leaving the cockles in sea water until you need them.

Cockles make good hookbaits when fishing for species like dabs or whiting. When fishing for dabs use a small hook, such as a freshwater size 6. The angler can thread three or four cockles on to the hook and present a reasonably sized bait.

Although cockles are a good bait by themselves, they are more widely used to tip the hook when using other baits such as lugworms or ragworms, which appeal to a much wider variety of fish.

Hooking Cockles

As they are a very small bait it is necessary to use several cockles on the hook at once if they are to have any impact at all.

Simply prsze open the shell and remove the contents. Thread the cockle on to the hook and push it up to the eye of the hook. Repeat the process until you have completely filled the hook. The last cockle should be put on to allow the hook to be pushed into the small orange foot. This is a much tougher part of the flesh and will help to keep the bait on the hook.

Ragworm

There are four members of the ragworm family that the sea angler uses for bait: the king ragworm, the white ragworm, the harbour rag or maddy, and the red ragworm. Harbour rags or maddies are the smallest of the ragworms and tend to be used when mullet or flounders are the main quarry. Red ragworm are the most commonly found of the four and are an excellent summer bait for both bass and flatfish.

The two most popular types of ragworm the sea angler is likely to use are the king rag and white ragworm. The king ragworm is the most widely used and can be bought from tackle shops or dug by the angler from the sea shore. It is possible to dig king ragworm that have grown to some 2 ft (60 cm) in length. However, the average size is around 14 in (35.6 cm), and the angler should take care when handling the king ragworm, as it has a pair of sharp pincers located within the mouth. These pincers are thrust out and retracted at random and can inflict a painful bite. Anglers digging their own worms are advised to seek out an area of sea shore close to the low water mark for digging. A garden fork and a bucket to keep the worms in will be needed. Estuaries can provide good numbers of king ragworm from a short period of digging in the shingle-type mud at low water. When walking over an area looking for signs of the ragworm, watch the surface of the mud for small jets of water spouting upward as the burrow is compressed under foot.

Some ragworms bury themselves deep and it may be necessary to dig down 2 ft (60 cm) or more. For long-term storage, ragworms may be kept in a shallow tank of sea water fitted with an air pump. Make sure you remove any damaged or dying worms, or the whole stock of worms will be ruined. If you are going to use them the next day, store them in newspaper in a fridge. It is advisable to change the newspaper after a few hours to make sure the worms are dry. This toughens up the skin and helps keep them on the hook longer. Ragworms should be used alive.

The white ragworm is much smaller in size than the king ragworm and, as the name suggests, it is creamy white or pale brown in colour. Much prized by the shore match

angler it can be gathered in the same manner as the king ragworm. They are more likely to be found living in softer sand or light shingle, usually in sheltered bays or similar areas. They seldom exceed 8 in (20 cm) in length and are easier to dig as they lie just under the surface. When collected, they can be kept in a plastic container in a shallow covering of sea water. The white ragworm is a very delicate worm and care should be taken when threading it on to the hook. As with the king ragworm, it is no good for freezing and should be used alive.

Hooking Ragworm

Large king ragworms should be threaded up the shank of the hook by passing the point of the hook through the centre of the ragworm. The head of the worm is pushed up over the eye of the hook and up on to the line above it. The lower body is held in place on the shank of the hook, and the tail is left hanging from the bend. Fine wire hooks are a good pattern to use when hooking any ragworm, as they allow an easy passage through the body. Smaller ragworms, like the harbour rag, can be hooked in bunches of four or five in the same manner until the hook is full. These make a good summer bait for mullet.

TOP: Ragworms and lugworms can be dug from the shore line or purchased from the tackle shop. They should be stored wrapped in newspaper in a cool place. If you are not going to use them straight away, examine them carefully; any dead or dying worms should be removed.

ABOVE LEFT: When hooking ragworms, the hook should be worked right through the centre of the worm, and the head should be worked up over the eye of the hook. A piece of squid can be used to tip the hook and hold the worm in place as shown. This is a very good bait for plaice and other flatfish.

ABOVE RIGHT: For flatfish such as plaice or flounders, a cocktail of ragworm and peeler crab is often a deadly bait. They should be mounted on the hook together as shown.

RIGHT: Bigger ragworm like the king rag can be used whole on the hook and should be threaded up the hook like this. To hook the worm, thread the hook through the centre of the worm, starting at the head end, and work the hook through the body, pushing the worm up the line. Leave the tail dangling.

Limpets

Limpets can be found in great numbers clinging to the rocks once the tide has dropped. This free bait is often overlooked by the sea angler, but during a storm, or directly after, they can be a top fish catcher. This is because many of them will have been washed from the rocks and will be rolling free in the surf. Species such as bass and flatfish will be among the first to pick up this free meal.

There are two types of limpet to be found along the British shore line. One is the common limpet; the other is the slipper limpet. The common limpet is the smaller of the two, reaching a size of 2 in (5 cm) across the shell. It can be found in great colonies, stuck to the rocky shores. The shell is dome-shaped, and the meat within is fitted with a suction pad at the base for clamping the limpet on to rocks.

The slipper, or American limpet, is not native to Britain. It appeared along the shores of Britain by accident and is thought to have arrived here among gravel imported from the United States. Slipper limpets can be found buried in shale and shingle, often near to white ragworm beds. They are larger in size than the common limpet and resemble a large mussel. They are a good bait for flounders and dabs. To collect limpets for bait, you will need a sharp knife and a bucket to store them in. When you have found a patch of limpets, insert the knife carefully under the side of the domed shell, twisting it to one side. This will allow air to enter the underside of the shell and force the limpet to retract, resulting in a loss of suction. Limpets are best used fresh from the shell, but if you find you have taken more than you need for a day's fishing, they can be salted and frozen. Adding salt to them before freezing helps to preserve them and toughens up the flesh.

Hooking Limpets

Of the two types, the slipper limpet is the more favoured for a hookbait. It is slightly softer in the flesh than the common and is and brighter in colour. Once removed from the shell, insert the hook twice into the flesh above the tough, fleshy foot. Once you have done this, take the point of the hook into the foot. Hooking in this manner will ensure the limpet stays on the

ABOVE: Limpets can be found clinging to rocks on and around the beach and make an excellent bait for flatfish. Once scooped out of the shell, they can be put on to the hook two or three at a time.

hook. For small species, such as dabs, you will only need to use one limpet on a small hook, probably a size 6. When fishing for bass or wrasse, it is advisable to fill a larger seahook like a 1/0 or 2/0 with at least half a dozen.

Limpets are a good bait to use when tipping the hook. Indeed, one of the best combinations to use for catching cod and dabs is a lugworm and limpet cocktail.

Mussels

Another shellfish bait that can be easily gathered from the sea shore is the mussel. They can be gathered by the angler from the rocks as the tide drops away to reveal them. The mussel is easily identified by the blue-black, elongated shell and is found in great clusters around jetty piles and on rocks. There are eight different varieties of mussel found around the British coast. The angler is most likely to use just two of them: the common mussel and the horse mussel. Once the meat is removed from the shell, the hook should be passed through the tougher flesh several times to make sure it stays on. This is a good bait to use when inshore boat fishing as the soft bait can be lowered into the water instead of being cast. If cast from the beach, the mussel may slip the hook due to its softness, unless it is bound with sheering elastic. Due to the soft nature of the flesh, many sea anglers now freeze the mussel bait on the rig they are going to use. Doing this provides the angler with a solid bait that can be cast a fair distance. Once in the water and in position on the sea bed the mussel bait will slowly defrost, but will remain intact on the hook. This is an excellent method for

BELOW: Mussels are a popular shellfish bait, easy to gather from the shore, and provide the angler with a good, all-round, cheap bait.

catching winter cod and codling when distance casting is a requirement.

To store mussels keep them in the bottom of a fridge at a cool temperature. It is advisable to wrap them in a cloth soaked in sea water, keeping the cloth damp at all times. If this is done properly, they can be kept like this for a week or more. To open them without damaging the flesh a knife with a ground edge will be necessary. It is not advisable to use a sharp, pointed blade as this could slip off the shell and cut the angler's hand.

A short blade with a rounded edge can be inserted into the groove where the two halves of the shell meet. Once in, the blade is twisted around, forcing the shell apart. Take your time in doing this, for if a shell is forced too hard the mussel inside will be damaged, leaving a handful of mushy gunge that will be useless as a bait.

Hooking Mussels

Because they are a soft bait it is necessary to get a good hook hold by threading a mussel well up the shank. It should be hooked as many times as possible in the tougher skin, working the hook through and through until a good hold is achieved.

If you are using fresh from the shell it is a good idea to bind the bait to the hook using elasticized cotton. This will hold it on the hook while it is being cast. Two or three mussels on a hook make a good bait for cod and pollack, especially when fishing from a boat.

As with other shellfish the mussel makes an excellent tipping bait.

Fished with a ragworm or squid, it is one of the top baits for plaice.

Other Baits

There are a number of other baits available for the sea angler to use. Every sea angler must experiment to find the bait that he or she prefers and also those that are readily available. Cost enters into it as it does to everything, but often the baits you can find around the sea shore or those that can be purchased cheaply are just as good as the more expensive offerings bought from tackle shops.

Preparing Hermit Crabs

1 **Hermit crabs live under stones and rocks and live ones make a good bass bait. Once extracted from the shell the crab should be used whole. Gently ease the hermit crab out of its shell in one piece, and it is then ready to be used as a bait.**

2 **Mount the hermit crab on a large single hook. They can also be used in conjunction with ragworm as a bait for cod and flatfish.**

Hermit Crabs

Hermit crabs make excellent baits and can often be found in rocks around the shore. They are particularly good for bass and should be used whole as described below.

Herring

Herring is another bait that is generally readily available from the fishmonger and is most effective for both conger eels and ling. The herring is a very oily fish and gives off a powerful odour that is attractive to predators and scavengers.

Preparing Herring

1 Herrings make a good, cheap bait, and the flesh is very oily. Cut a whole herring into chunks like this.

2 Use the chunks as a single bait or try two or three chunks on a larger hook for conger eels and ling.

Artificial Baits

Artificial baits are often a good alternative to fresh bait, especially for the boat angler. Because of the way in which the tidal flow moves, an artificial bait such as a Redgill sandeel can be made to look much like the real thing. Many shore anglers derive endless hours of sport from the use of spinners or plugs. For the inshore dinghy angler a baited spoon for flounder fishing is a top method when drifting in a running tide. There are a host of different artificials available to the sea angler for both shore and boat fishing, and they can be placed in several different categories. The categories are: spinners, spoons, feathers, plugs (both sinking and floating), rubber eels, pirks (for wreck fishing), jelly worms and even rubber squid, called muppets. With so much choice it is often difficult to decide which is best. All the above artificial lures are used by both boat and shore anglers. Some of the more specialist items, such as plugs, are the tools of the specialist bass angler. Whichever you choose to try, they all have their place in sea angling.

ABOVE: A traditional spinner used mainly for mackerel but which has taken other species. Spinners, which revolve rapidly on their own axis, have reflective panels that shine as they are retrieved through the water and mimic the action of smaller fish.

ABOVE: Pollack and coalfish are prime targets of the artificial bait angler. Specimens like this can be caught using pirks and rubber eels.

Spinners

Spinners come in many shapes and sizes and are usually made from metal. They are more commonly used by shore anglers fishing for pollack and mackerel. The weight of the spinner aids casting and will sink the spinner down into the depths of the sea. Once cast, the angler can count the spinner down to the bottom to determine the depth. On or near the bottom, the spinner is retrieved by winding it back on a slow or fast wind of the reel. The slower the retrieve,

the deeper the spinner will fish. To fish the upper layers of the water a faster retrieve will be needed to keep the spinner from sinking too deep. The angler should also try to vary the speed of retrieve. This will make the spinner behave in an erratic way and resemble a small fish in distress. Using this method is usually the key to enticing a passing fish to strike at it.

Spinners are available in a wide variety of sizes and colours. Among the more popular designs is the range including the famous Toby and Krill designs, well used by thousands of shore anglers up and down the coast. Smaller round-bladed spinners are usually used for tempting species such as thin-lipped mullet. When using a small-bladed spinner it is a good idea to tip the hook with a fresh bait like ragworm. This adds to the spinner's attraction and will tempt several species. Bigger bar-shaped spinners can be used for pollack or bass. Probably the most popular type for the shore angler is the small- to medium-weight, elongated variety used for mackerel.

Spinners are usually silver, gold or bronze in colour and will often have a reflective panel on each side. This reflective surface shines when it is caught by the light rays penetrating the sea's surface as the spinner is being retrieved. At the front end of the spinner, where it is tied to the line, is a split ring, to which a swivel is fitted. The swivel allows the spinner to rotate freely and move with ease as it is retrieved through the water, and it prevents line twist. The back end of the spinner is also fitted with a split ring, to which a treble hook is attached. A treble hook is used to ensure a good hook hold, as the attacking fish will be taking the spinner while it is on the move. The use of a single hook would be impractical, as it could be missed by the fish as it attacks the spinner.

Plain spinners can be decorated with a stick-on metallic strip called Flectolite. This is often a good way of improving an otherwise dull-looking lure. Spinners can be used from the boat, especially when fishing in the mouth of an estuary over sand banks. Species like mackerel and bass will provide good sport for the boat angler using a balanced, light-line approach with a proven pattern of spinner.

When to Use

If the mackerel are shoaling on or near the surface they will probably be chasing fry. This is a good opportunity to use a small- to medium-weight silver spinner.

Top Tip

Counting the spinner down through the water at a rate of 12 in (30.5 cm) per second, and varying the depths at which you start the retrieve, will give you an indication of the depth the fish are swimming at when you get a take.

Silver and gold spoons

Spoons

Spoons are rather a specialist item of tackle and tend to be used by the sea angler when fishing for flatfish. As the name suggests, the shape is that of a spoon, and some sea anglers make their own from old metal spoons. They are available from tackle shops in two varieties, metal and plastic, in sizes from 2–4 in (5–10 cm) in length.

ABOVE: Spoons are often used with the addition of a baited hook. As the spoon flutters over the sand and silt the movement imitates a small crab scurrying for cover.

The plastic variety is produced in a number of different colours, including orange, yellow and white, while metal spoons can be made more attractive by tipping the edges with red or white paint. However, a custom-built, home-made version with a string of attractor beads may well out-fish a shop-bought spoon. It is the boat angler who will benefit most from using spoons, as they are easier to work in the tide from a boat and will require little or no weight.

Species such as flounder, plaice and turbot can all be tricked by the fluttering movement of a spoon as it rotates in the tidal flow. Like the spinner, some spoons have a split ring fitted at each end. A small swivel is fitted to each split ring, allowing the spoon to rotate as it is retrieved. One

RIGHT: Dabs, plaice and flounder are all prime candidates for the spoon angler.

of the swivels is tied to the main line, and a short length of 10 lb (4.54 kg) line some 6 in (15 cm) long is tied to the other line. To the end of this a hook is attached, usually a long shank, fine wire, size 1 or similar. The addition of a few coloured beads on the hook length gives the spoon that vital bit of added attraction.

Another version of the spoon rig is where the spoon is threaded on to a central axis at the narrow end only. A weight is fitted below and the hook is attached further down. This method of attachment allows the spoon to rotate around the axis, disturbing the sand and mud with the larger end of the blade. This imitates a small flatfish trying to escape and is a good presentation for turbot.

With either method the hook is baited with ragworm, lugworm or crab bait. As the spoon moves across the bottom with the tide, it sends up small clouds of sand and mud. This suggests to any nearby flatfish that a small crab or prawn is scurrying over the sand. Once spotted, the hungry flatfish moves in for the kill and is hooked in the process. Another reason for the spoon's great catching ability is said to be that bigger flatfish look upon the spoon as a small flatfish, trying to run off with a piece of bait. In an effort to stop this supposed smaller fish, the spoon is often hit quite hard by a larger specimen.

An important note to bear in mind when using a spoon is to fish it with the tidal flow. This is due to the fact that flounder, in particular, feed and swim with the flow. Spoons can also be used from the shore, but it will be necessary to add weight to the spoon if it is to be cast any distance. If weight is added this should be done in the form of a barrel lead or series of small ball weights that can be fitted on to the central axis.

When to Use

Spoons are, in the right hands, more effective than a static bait and should be used at every opportunity, especially if flounder are the quarry.

Top Tip

If making your own spoons or buying shop-bought patterns, it's good practice to add plenty of colourful beads to the trace below the spoon. These beads will give the spoon an extra attraction.

Plugs

Over the past few years plugs have become the main method of attack for many a specialist bass angler, but they can be used for pollack, coalfish and mackerel as well. Plugs come in two different forms: sinking and floating. They are machine-made from plastic or hand-crafted from wood and are constructed either as a single or as a jointed-body version. Many are coloured in a wide variety of different designs. Some have eyes painted on, while others have stick-on bubble eyes with a moving eyeball. When selecting your plugs, be careful not to get caught yourself, as many are designed to catch anglers and not fish.

The jointed-body versions give extra movement and wobble violently when retrieved through the water. They are designed to mimic smaller species and have the ability to deceive fish into taking them if fished properly. As the plug is on the move, the hunting fish has only a split second as it passes across its line of vision to decide whether to take it or not. When the take occurs, it is usually quite savage, as the hunting fish will hit the target to kill.

Of the two types in use, the bass angler is likely to place more faith in the floating patterns. Floating plugs float on the surface when cast, but when retrieved at speed will dive under the surface as they are worked back to the rod. The front of the plug is usually fitted with a plastic vane or lip, which when hit by water pressure forces the plug down or up, depending on the angle at which the vane or lip is set. A floating plug is a good choice over rocky or weedy ground, as it is not so easy to lose on snags or rocks.

Sinking plugs are built in a similar fashion, but as the name suggests, they sink. This is due to extra weight in the body, plus additional weight, such as a metal insert or heavy lip positioned at the head of the plug. Sinking and floating plugs will catch bass, mackerel and even pollack, and some great sport can be had fishing with them on light tackle.

One of the top plugs in use for bass fishing is the Rapala Silver. Many bass anglers favour the jointed-body version, which is a very good imitation of a large sandeel. The Silver is coloured with a blue back and a silvery-white underside.

When fishing with both types it is important to make the plug work for you. This is achieved by varying the speed of retrieve and working the rod tip from side to side as you wind in the line. Although more effective from the shore, plugs do have their place on the boat. They can be effective for larger pollack and coalfish when wreck fishing.

When to Use

If in search of big bass, try a floating plug fished at the mouth of an estuary. Bass will wait here for the tide to turn so they can ambush any smaller fish leaving the river.

Top Tip

Many plugs come fitted with small, inferior treble hooks. It's a good idea to remove these and replace them with a larger, stronger pattern.

Pirks

Pirks are used by boat anglers for catching cod, pollack and ling when fishing over wrecks or rough ground. A pirk is basically a cylindrical metal tube of varying length. It is heavy enough to sink down to the bottom under its own weight, so no additional lead on the line is required.

Many boat anglers make their own pirks from lengths of chrome tubing. A quantity of lead is poured into the centre of the tubing giving weight to the finished pirk. This enables the angler to get the pirk down to the wreck faster, especially in a strong tide. At each end of the pirk a large split ring is fitted by drilling a hole so the ring can be threaded on to the main body. A large treble hook is fitted to one end, a swivel to the other. The swivel is used to tie the pirk to the main line. The pirk can then be decorated by using a stick-on metallic strip, called Flectolite. This will add a touch of sparkle to the pirk as it is being worked over a wreck.

Although pirks can be bought in tackle shops, they tend to be on the expensive side considering their simple construction. Many of the commercially produced pirks have the added attraction of a muppet or plastic skirt fitted to the hook. When

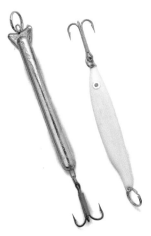

ABOVE: These large, heavy pirks are for fishing off deep-water wrecks. They can be used as they are, or additional bait can be tipped on to the hook.

LEFT: This brightly coloured wrasse has fallen for the charms of a plug that was intended for bass.

ABOVE: **A pirk can be used to provide the weight when using muppet lures.**

used over a deep-water mark, big fish will be attracted to the silver flash as the pirk is worked up and down in the tide. They will home in on its movement thinking it is a smaller fish. Some anglers use a pirk in place of a weight when fishing with a team of feathers. This increases their chances even further as a larger specimen may take the pirk in preference to the feathers. Pirks can be made or bought in various sizes. The bigger ones, weighing upward of 1 lb (0.45 kg), are used for deep water and strong tides. Some of the smaller models are bent or kinked in the centre to make them wobble as they are brought back towards the surface. Small pirks with a kink in them are often used in shallower water where bass may be present.

When to Use
Every boat angler who is fishing over a wreck should have a pirk in his or her tackle box. There are days when big cod will look at nothing else.

Top Tip
Big ling are often caught on a pirk baited with squid or mackerel.

Feathers
Feathers come in many different colours and sizes, from mixed red, yellow and blue, to plain white and even silver foil. The most common type available are the sets of multi-coloured feathers. These are usually fished in sets of three, four, six or twelve. From the boat or off the shore, feathers are a primary lure when mackerel fishing.

The idea behind a set of feathers is to create a simulated shoal of small fry that mackerel and pollack in

particular will pursue. When shore fishing, the feathers are cast out as far as you can get them. They are then wound back to the rod in a jerking fashion to draw attention.

Mackerel feathers can be bought ready-tied from a tackle shop. They will consist of different colours and be tied to a smallish seahook, usually a 1/0. At each end of the trace there will be a loop. The two loops are for joining a weight at one end and a swivel at the other. To join the weight or swivel, pass the loop through the eye of the swivel or loop of the weight and then take the swivel or weight back through the loop. When fishing from a boat for mackerel it is better to use a set of six feathers. Using any more may result in a tangle when you hook a full house.

Using a six-hook trace for mackerel can soon result in plenty of fresh bait for other species when out on the

boat. Larger white feathers in sets of three or six are used by cod, ling and bass anglers. For some reason, cod in particular seem to have a preference for white. Cod feathers are tied on bigger hooks, usually a size 4/0 to 6/0. If needed, the hooks can be tipped with a piece of fresh mackerel to give them an added attraction.

When to Use
It's always worth trying a set of feathers from a boat, especially when catching mackerel for bait. If cod are the target make sure you have a trace of big white feathers available.

Top Tip
Many commercially made feathers are too long, with too many feathers whipped to the hook. This can result in short takes. Take a pair of scissors and trim down the feathers so that the hook shows clearly.

TOP: **Feathers can be used six or twelve at a time for catching large numbers of mackerel from a boat.**

ABOVE: **A new generation of feather imitations has been introduced on to the market. These imitation feathers are made from soft plastics and are very bright and work particularly well.**

LEFT: **This pirk is being used in conjunction with a muppet skirt and bait.**

Artificial Eels

As the name suggests, these imitation sandeels are constructed to mimic the real thing. Artificial eels are killer lures for such species as pollack, bass and coalfish and are catchers of large species when fished over a wreck from a boat. Made from materials such as latex or rubber, these deadly imitations are fitted with a hook that is tied on to a trace running through the centre of the body.

The two main attractions of artificial eels are the colour and the incredibly lifelike tail. On most models the tail is made of a flimsy thin rubber, which incorporates a small but sensitive rudder at the tip. When retrieved through the water, the rudder is forced from side to side, making the tail wobble in the tide. It is this movement that brings the artificial eel to life.

Artificial eels are effective from both shore and boat. However, it's the bigger patterns that tend to be used when boat fishing over a wreck and the smaller ones for rock, pier and jetty work. Eels as large as 15 in (38 cm) in length are standard wreck tackle for the boat angler. These are fished on a flying collar rig. This involves the use of a long 15 lb (6.8 kg) trace, 15–20 ft (4.57–6.1 m) in length. One end of the trace is tied to a boom, which stands out of the main line. The other end of the trace is

ABOVE: A good selection of rubber eels will be needed when fishing over a wreck.

threaded through the nose of the eel and out through the underside at the beginning of the tail. A hook is then tied to the trace, and the trace and hook are pulled back into position inside the eel's body. The lead, which may be as heavy as 8 oz (227 g), is tied on a weak link of line directly under the bottom of the boom. The weak link of line should be of a breaking strain lower than 6 lb (2.72 kg). This is so that the lead can break away from the rig, leaving the

ABOVE: An artificial eel accounted for this fine pollack, caught over a wreck.

eel intact if the angler gets caught up on the wreck.

When sent down to the wreck in a running tide, the artificial eel sits out away from the boom in the tidal flow. The tidal flow works the eel's tail, making it look natural. From the shore, the smaller types are good lures to use for bass and pollack when fishing at night.

These work really well if the sea is calm. This is because species like bass are able to pick up on the vibration caused by the tail as the eel is wound in. Colours for both boat and shore are a matter of personal choice. However, over the years a few colours have gained great popularity. Boat anglers in particular favour black, orange or red. There are many different makes of artificial eel available, but two designs in particular have probably

ABOVE: The line runs through the centre of the eel and is tied to a hook that sits inside the body of the eel. Once on the move, the rubber tail sways in the flow and looks just like the real thing.

accounted for more captures of specimen fish than any other makes. These are the Redgill and the Eddystone eels. Both are constructed from rubber and have a flexible tail, which moves when worked in the tide's flow. They are available in different colours and in sizes from 3–18 in (7.5–45 cm).

When to Use

From the shore a small black artificial fished at dusk around rocky ground will attract bass. From a boat the bigger patterns are regarded as standard wreck fare.

Top Tip

When buying artificial eels some of the patterns have too heavy a gauge hook fitted. Remove this and replace it with a fine wire pattern. This will ensure that the eel acts as naturally as possible.

Muppets

Muppets are another example of a rubber lure that catch their fair share of sea species. They are sold in packs of three or six, loose or ready-tied to a trace. There are three sizes to choose from: small, medium and large. Like other artificials the muppet is also available in a multitude of colours. Among the most popular are the fluorescent green, red and black patterns favoured by boat anglers for pollack and cod. In the smaller sizes, which are around 3 in (7.5 cm) in length, they can be used on a trace of three, with the lead fixed beneath them. The medium size, approximately 6 in (15 cm) in length, is a good pattern to try added to the hook of a pirk. Red is a top catching colour when using this method; cod in particular seem to home in on this combination. Medium-sized muppets are also good for fishing as a trio when the hooks are tipped with mackerel strip. The largest size of muppet is around 12 in (30 cm) in length and is used as a single lure.

There are two main ways of attaching a muppet to the hook. The first is correct when using a small or medium-sized muppet with a single hook. The point of the single hook is simply inserted into the dome at the tip of the head, pushed through the rubber, and the point brought round and under the skirt of tentacles. When ready to fish, the point of the hook needs to be exposed from one side of the muppet to ensure a good hook hold when the fish takes.

When using on a pirk which has a treble hook fitted, a small hole will have to be cut in the tip of the head of the muppet. The hook should then be

ABOVE: Muppets are available in all sizes and colours. Some of the more popular makes have a glitter effect on the body. This acts as an attractor when caught in the light.

removed from the pirk and the eye of the treble hook worked back through the hole. The three points of the hook should sit under the muppet skirt with the points protruding. The hook is then clipped back on to the pirk, and the deadly combination is ready for fishing. Muppets can be fished in two different ways.

The first is to let the tide do the work for you if you are fishing from a boat in a tidal run. It's simply a case of lowering the muppets down near the bottom and letting them wave about in the tide.

The second requires a little bit of work from the angler. With little or no tide movement it is important to keep muppets on the move and it is necessary to work the muppets up and down to draw attention. This is done by lifting and lowering the rod tip as the muppets are retrieved.

Muppets of all sizes can account for some bumper hauls of pollack and cod when fishing over wrecks or rough ground. They can be used from the shore just as effectively, and the smaller sizes, fished in a team of three, can account for some action from pollack and bass.

When to Fish
No wreck angler worth his salt should contemplate a fishing trip without an assortment of muppets in his tackle box. Try jigging a team of three up from the bottom when pollack or cod are the target species.

Top Tip
When the tide runs slow, jig the rod tip up and down and this will make the muppets work as they are brought up from the depths. When sport is slow it can often pay to bait the muppets with squid strips. This tactic often produces a fish and is a deadly combination for big ling.

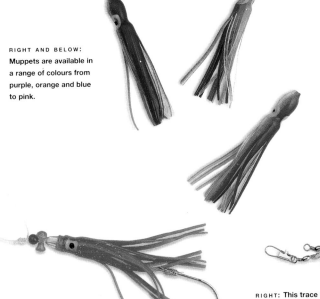

RIGHT AND BELOW: Muppets are available in a range of colours from purple, orange and blue to pink.

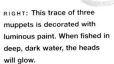

RIGHT: This trace of three muppets is decorated with luminous paint. When fished in deep, dark water, the heads will glow.

Jellies and Twisters

Jellies and twister lures have become a big part of sea angling over the past few years. Imported from the United States, this new breed of soft rubber lure is at home on the boat or from the shore. There are hundreds of different designs and patterns to choose from. Jelly lures have a worm-shaped body and are usually impregnated with a colourful glitter pattern and fish-catching smell. The worm is very soft and flexible and will often have a built-in tail action to tantalize and tease fish into striking at it. As a rule, the worms tend to be unweighted, and it is merely a case of inserting a sharp seahook, such as a 1/0 or 2/0.

When hooking, they should be treated in a similar manner as a live worm, with the hook threaded down through the centre of the worm's head and exiting at the side, a short distance from the entry point. From the shore they can be fished for bass, pollack and mackerel. Lighter colours tend to work better from the shore during the day as they resemble sandeels, a favourite food of these species. After dark, the colour is not that important, as the predator relies on vibration and shape to find its target. The smaller variety can be fished on a three-hook trace from the boat and it is extremely effective for species such as pollack and coalfish.

Leadheads or twister lures are a weighted lure. As the name suggests, the twister lure works on the principle of a twisting tail in order to attract the predator fish.

These are made from soft rubber and have a double tail fin that twists on the retrieve. Shore anglers and boat anglers catch many different species using this type of lure. Because they are weighted they are a good choice for the shore angler: there will be no need to add any additional lead to the line for casting.

With a separate leadhead section the angler is free to choose any colour tail he or she wishes to use and can vary it at will during the day. A real bonus with this system is that the tail can be changed easily, and the angler does not have to break down the complete rig to do so.

LEFT: This large leadhead lure is ready to be dropped into the depths. Species like bass, pollack, coalfish and cod will all take such a lure.

ABOVE: Red gill eels also have a twister tail action when retrieved.

BELOW: A selection of leadhead lures showing the different sizes available.

Many of the original leadhead twister lures are designed to fish with the hook positioned upside down. This is a good point to watch out for when buying them as this pattern will rarely snag on the bottom over rocky ground. If you browse through the pages of any sea-angling magazine you will see companies in America advertising every kind of rubber twister lure available.

When to Use

The original Mr Twister lures with the leadhead are a must for the shore angler in search of pollack and bass. Fish them over rocks and rough ground on the high tide or just as the tide starts to drop. Leadhead lures also account for some huge catches of ling over the wrecks in the Irish Sea.

Top Tip

If you keep getting hit on a jellyworm but can't hook the fish, cut 1 in (2.5 cm) from the head and re-hook the worm. It could be that the worm is too long for the species chasing it.

Shore Fishing

For a great number of sea anglers, fishing from the shore is where it all begins. Many start as young children on holiday who have been taken mackerel fishing on the local pier. Armed with borrowed tackle, a string of brightly coloured feathers and the promise of a fresh mackerel for dinner, that first day out by the sea is a treasured one that will be remembered forever. Once that first fish is hooked, so too, is the angler – invariably for life.

Various Coastlines

The coastlines of Britain and other countries are full of opportunities for the shore angler to explore. From beach to rock fishing, piers, breakwater walls and the countless numbers of estuaries, there is a whole host of venues to choose from.

The species of fish the angler wishes to pursue will often determine the location he or she is likely to choose. Wide, sandy beaches are a top spot for summer ray fishing. Piers and jetties attract shoals of mullet and mackerel. Rocky headlands provide sport from bass, wrasse and dogfish.

Breakwater walls often give deep water and can offer the chance of a large conger eel if you are prepared to fish at night. The estuary angler will find rich pickings when the winter flounder fishing is in full swing or casting from the beach for codling.

This section deals with everything from the most appropriate choice of rod and reel, right down to that all-important hook and how to present it. It offers advice on the various locations and how to choose suitable tackle and methods for the species you are fishing, with plenty of tips and tactics.

Whichever venue you choose and whatever species you fish for, ensure a future for your sport by unhooking undersized fish carefully and returning them to the sea.

ABOVE: A successful day's fishing for the shore angler.

BELOW: The sun slips away as two beach anglers wait for action.

Equipment

With so many different makes of rods, reels and lines in the tackle shops, it's often a daunting task for the shore angler, especially the beginner, to make the correct choice.

Rods

Rods for shore fishing will vary in length depending on the type of fishing they are going to be used for. Spinning rods can be anything from 6–10 ft (1.83–3.05 m) in length; pier rods are usually around 10 ft (3.05 m) and can be used for leger and float work, and beachcasters are almost always 12 ft (3.66 m) or in some cases 13 ft (3.96 m) long. Other types of rod that can be used are freshwater rods, such as light carp or float rods. These models play key roles in specialist bass and mullet fishing. However, in general, most sea anglers choose a 12 ft (3.66 m) beach rod that can be used from a beach, a pier, an estuary or from rocks for many different applications, including legering and even float fishing.

A beachcaster is usually made up of two 6 ft (1.83 m) pieces, a tip section and a butt section. The butt section is the lower end of the rod, which houses the reel. It is important to use a rod of at least 12 ft (3.66 m) as this will increase the casting ability. There are several factors to take into account when purchasing a beachcaster. First, there is the type of reel you are going to use with it; second, there is cost; and third, there is the type of fishing you are going to use it for and what material the rod is made of.

The reel you intend to use will have a great bearing on the selection of the rod. There are two types of reel in common use among sea anglers: fixed-spool and multiplier reels. When buying a rod to match up with a fixed-spool reel, you will find the design differs from a rod used in conjunction with a multiplier reel.

The rings on a rod for fixed-spool reels will be larger in size and will number four or five in total, including the tip ring. It is common to find all the guides only on the tip section of the rod with nothing on the butt section apart from the reel seating. The four or five guides should be large in circumference around the inner ring, decreasing in size towards the tip ring. This is because when casting with a fixed-spool reel, the guides on the rod need to allow a clear passage of non-friction to the line as it leaves the reel. Since the line is coiled as it leaves the reel, fewer rings on the rod allows for a smooth, unhindered cast. On a beach rod to be matched with a multiplier reel the opposite applies.

There can be as many as nine guides of a much smaller size and inner-ring circumference. There is usually one guide on the butt section of the rod with the other seven or eight, including the tip ring, whipped on to the tip section. Once again, the guides are dictated by the way in which the line leaves the reel.

In the case of the multiplier reel, the line leaves in a free motion from a revolving spool. Due to the speed it releases from the spool, the small guides are needed to pull the line down quickly towards the rod blank, keeping it in-line with the action of the rod. On the cast, as the line travels down the guides, each one gets smaller towards the tip, pulling the line down quickly to the blank. This gives better control and reduces stress on the line.

For the beginner, the better choice for a first rod would be a model suited to a fixed-spool reel. For the more experienced angler who has mastered casting, a rod with rings for a multiplier is usually the choice. Both types of beach rod will have different actions, and this is an important factor when choosing a rod for the type of fishing you are going to do.

Shore anglers who need to cast a bait a fair distance to reach the fish will need to look at models that are stiffer in the butt and middle, but have a softer tip. This type of rod has what is called a fast taper, and will very much aid distance casting. The stiffer lower and middle sections will transmit power through the rod during the cast. The softer tip will allow good bite detection when fishing.

If distance is not required a through-action rod is more suitable. This type of rod bends progressively from the top of the butt to the tip. With regard to cost and materials used to manufacture rods, the best advice would be to save for a decent carbon rod capable of doing what is required. There are a lot of cheaper rods around made from fibreglass and composite (glass and low-grade carbon mixed). They break very easily if pushed beyond their casting limits, leaving the angler to pay out for another rod.

Many of the more expensive rods are made from high grades of carbon. However, they do cost much more. Nevertheless, there are many

ABOVE: A pair of distance casting rods complete with multiplier reels.

RIGHT: This rod is for use with a multiplier reel. It also has an extension butt so that the reel can be positioned further down the handle.

examples of good-quality carbon beach rods starting at reasonable prices that will do all they proclaim and are long-lasting.

There are a couple of things you should do when purchasing a rod. Look at the butt of the rod you are thinking of buying as it should have a maximum casting weight printed on it. This will help you with your choice as it will tell you about the casting ability of the rod. It may also pay to take your reel along to the shop. Try this fitted on to the rod and see if it feels comfortable and balanced. Only when you are satisfied that you have the correct rod for the job should you make your purchase.

Fixed-spool Reels

As with rods, there is a vast array of reels for the shore angler to choose from. The two main reels in use are the fixed-spool and the multiplier. The fixed-spool is the easier to use and a sensible choice for the beginner. For shore fishing from the beach, pier or rocks the fixed-spool reel needs to be large enough to hold a good capacity of line and robust enough to deal with casting heavy weights.

The reel is fixed to the rod by inserting it into the reel seat on the butt of the rod. For the fixed-spool reel this is on the underside of the rod. The line is loaded on to a cone-shaped spool and when cast, leaves the reel in coil form, travelling up through the rod guides. You should be able to load at least 150 yds (137 m) of 20 lb (9.07 kg) line on to the reel. Most shore anglers use 15–18 lb (6.8–8.16 kg) main line and fill with line to just below the lip of the spool.

ABOVE: The fixed-spool beach reel, a good reel to learn to cast with.

When filling the spool make sure the line is evenly distributed, as this will help to prevent tangles when casting. It is crucial not to underfill or overfill the spool, as both will hinder smooth casting.

There is a mechanism called a bale arm on the outer edge of the reel. This traps the line and winds it around the spool when it is engaged and the reel handle is turned. When the bale arm is opened, the line is free to run from the spool. The bale arm on most models is automatically shut when the handle is turned after the cast has been made. Some anglers cut the bale arm right down to a bare minimum for tournament casting purposes. They do this to avoid the bale arm accidentally shutting and trapping the line during a long cast. Many models of fixed-spool reel offer an adaptable handle that can be

ABOVE: Many beginners to sea angling will start off using a fixed-spool reel because they are easier to use.

switched to the left- or right-hand side of the reel, depending on the angler. At the front of the reel there should be a tensioning nut at the head of the spool. This is called a drag system, and determines how tight or slack the spool is set. If set in a slack position, line can be pulled from the spool in a free movement, usually by a large fish when the angler is playing it. If set tight, no line will be allowed to run free. It's always advisable to pre-set the drag to suit the species you are likely to encounter. At the rear of the reel there is usually an anti-reverse switch. This is so that the angler can switch from forward to backward wind allowing him to yield line if not using the drag system.

Expect to pay anything from £39.99 up to £150 depending on the make

and model of reel you choose. For specialist fishing, when a light-line approach can be used, smaller models are more appropriate. Many sea anglers are turning to freshwater, fixed-spool carp reels when float fishing for mullet or plug fishing for bass.

Multipliers

Mention multipliers and a vast majority of shore anglers will tell you that they are the ultimate reel for distance casting. Several of the top casters use a multiplier when competing on the tournament casting circuit. Modern multipliers are now so light and small it's no wonder they are favoured by the distance caster over the heavier, fixed-spool reel.

Multiplier reels are very different in design from the fixed-spool reel. For a start, the spool, instead of being cone-shaped, is a drum shape. This revolves on a central axis within the reel's casing. The multiplier is mounted on the top side of the rod with the guides facing upward. It is either placed into a fixed reel seat or, in a few cases where extreme distance is required, it is fitted well down towards the end of the butt with special reel clips called coasters. With the reel positioned in the low butt position the angler is able to exert greater leverage through the rod as the cast is made.

One big problem the newcomer faces when using a multiplier reel is the overrunning of the spool during the cast. This can cause a terrible mess in the line, called a bird's nest. Overruns are caused by lack of braking control on the rotating spool as the lead touches down at the end of the cast. At this point of the cast, if your reel has no braking system, you will need to apply slight pressure with your thumb to prevent an overrun. Many modern multipliers have a built-in braking system in the form of either magnetic brakes or centrifugal brakes, which is a great help.

Magnetic brakes work on the principle of a magnet fixed opposite the spool end. This draws the side plate of the spool closer to slow it down. Alternatively, the magnet can be set further away to allow more freedom of movement. Centrifugal brakes are two small brake blocks fitted to a pin at the end of the spool. These blocks are forced to the end of the pin when the spool is in motion.

ABOVE: There are several different models of multiplier reels available. Make sure you make the right choice.

Once at the end they come into contact with a small metal loop in the side plate, causing friction. This, in turn, slows the spool down.

Several makes of multiplier have what is called a level-wind fitted to a bar running across the face of the reel. This little gadget ensures the line is retrieved back on to the reel evenly. It works when the handle is turned, moving from side to side across the reel, laying the line evenly for the next cast. Once the angler's casting has progressed, the level-wind can be removed to increase the distance of the cast. Looking down on the reel from above, a double handle is usually located at the right-hand side of the reel. Most of the models on the market today have the handles fitted on the right.

One point to consider when purchasing a multiplier is to buy one suited to the fishing you are likely to do. You may need to purchase two models, one for beach work and one for rough ground. The models vary in their design, and a small multiplier used for casting from a beach will be no good for heavy, rough-ground work. Prices for multipliers have evened out over the past years, and there are many good examples on sale. If you want the latest model, however, then you should be prepared to pay a little more.

Whatever model of reel you use, always rinse it under a tap when returning from a fishing trip, then place it somewhere warm, such as an airing cupboard, to dry. Saltwater is

ABOVE: When you visit any tackle shop, you will be met with a vast array of rods and reels to choose from. Ask your tackle dealer for advice when you are buying equipment for the first time.

extremely corrosive, and reels not washed in freshwater after fishing in the sea will quickly deteriorate.

Lines

There are several different brands of line on the market. Many make all sorts of claims to being the best available, being the most abrasive-resistant and having the lowest diameter for breaking strain. Take care when you are making a purchase that the line you have bought will be suited to the type of fishing you are going to do. It's pointless trying to fish over extremely rough ground for conger eels with a line of 15 lb (6.8 kg) breaking strain. If you don't snap the line on a snag, the first conger you hook will snap it for you. Look carefully at all the hazards you are likely to encounter before buying your line. When you have made your choice of breaking strain, select a well-known brand that has stood the test of time with other anglers. There are some very good lines on the market, and there are also some very bad ones. Go to a reputable dealer and tell him what you are looking for in a line. If he values your custom he will advise you correctly. Among some of the more popular brands are the tried and tested Sylcast line, Drennan Sea line and Daiwa Sea line. All are of good quality, are available in bulk spools and are reasonably priced.

Lines for shore fishing will vary in breaking strain in accordance with the species you are fishing for and the type of sea bed you are fishing over.

ABOVE: There is a wide variety of line available to the sea angler. The market place is extremely competitive with hundreds of different brands, colours and breaking strains.

As a rule, from the open beach the angler will usually use 15–18 lb (6.8–8.16 kg) breaking strain main line with a 50–60 lb (22.68–27.22 kg) shock leader. An angler fishing over rough ground will increase the strength of the main line to 35 lb (15.88 kg) to combat the rough seabed or rock he or she is fishing over. When in pursuit of bass and fishing with plugs or spinners, it is better to use a lighter line. A line with a breaking strain of 8–10 lb (3.63–4.54 kg) will allow the bait to behave more naturally and will allow smoother, longer casting, which is important.

It is important that shock leaders are used when punching heavy leads out at distance. A shock leader is a length of heavier line which is attached to the end of the main line. As the leader is heavier, the line is able to cope with the strain, and this avoids any unnecessary break-offs on the lighter main line. Shock leaders are usually coloured fluorescent yellow or orange. This helps the angler to see the line when fishing at night or when winding the lead back to the rod in rough conditions.

Line can be bought in bulk spools.

ABOVE: Line is available in a wide range of colours. Many anglers now prefer to use a fluorescent line because it is easier to see, particularly at night.

Loading a Leader for Casting

When you are using the pendulum cast to achieve maximum distance it is advisable to incorporate a leader. The leader is a stronger breaking strain line which acts as a shock absorber when the rod is fully compressed.

This leader line is usually a minimum of 50 lb (22.68 kg) breaking strain and approximately 18 ft (5.5 m) in length. When ready to cast, the leader will be hanging from the end of the rod with three or four turns on the reel. As the cast is made and the rod begins to compress, the strain is transmitted to this part of the line and prevents the main line breaking unnecessarily.

1 To load the leader on to the reel before casting first make sure the line on the spool is lying in a flat, even manner across the drum of the reel.

2 Wind on the leader, making sure that the leader joint knot is wound on at one end of the spool. Here it is on the right-hand side of the spool.

ABOVE: A long-distance caster needs a well-serviced reel and good quality shock leader material.

3 This avoids the knot catching on your thumb as the line leaves the spool. As the knot is tapered at one end it will be easily drawn up through the rod rings. Make sure the leader is wound on evenly.

4 This is how the line should be trapped before casting. Grip the rod tightly with one hand around the blank by the reel. Press your thumb firmly down on the leader to trap it until the release is made.

Terminal Tackle and Equipment Hooks

The shore angler will need several items of terminal tackle if he or she is to be successful in the pursuit of different species of sea fish. One key component is the hook. When choosing a hook it's important to think about the species and the bait. The hook needs to be strong enough to cope with the species, but it must

RIGHT: Hooks come in all shapes and sizes.

also be balanced to suit the bait. A basic rule is, the bigger the bait the bigger the hook. There are many patterns to choose from and the shore angler will need to arm him or herself with a wide variety to meet different situations. Most hooks are available in packets of ten or boxes of 50. It is a good idea to have a selection of sizes, from a size 4/0 through to a 6/0, of different patterns. These patterns and sizes should cover most shore situations the angler is likely to encounter.

The three main patterns used for shore angling are Aberdeen,

ABOVE: This box contains a good selection of hooks to cover every situation.

ABOVE: Long-shanked fine wire O'Shaughnessy and Aberdeen hooks in varying sizes.

O'Shaughnessy and Limerick hooks. Aberdeens are made in fine and thick wire gauges. This pattern is probably the most commonly used. For bigger fish, such as cod or conger eels, and when presenting a bigger bait, the O'Shaughnessy represents a good, strong hook and should be used.

ABOVE: A sharpening stone is a useful tool to take on a fishing trip.

For delicate baits, such as live sandeels, it is advisable to use a long shank, fine-wire Aberdeen hook. For species like mullet, dabs and sole, a small hook is the order of the day. The shore angler may do better to turn to the freshwater angler's tackle box, where sizes 6 and 8 short shank hooks are a good choice. Small baits, like bread flake for mullet and cockles for dabs, can be used to conceal the hook completely for these small-mouthed species. Limerick hooks are used for presenting larger bulky baits and are a good choice for the shore angler when fishing crab. The Limerick hook has a wider gape than the other two patterns, and this prevents the point of the hook being masked by the bait. When storing hooks, the shore angler should keep them in a watertight container as fine-

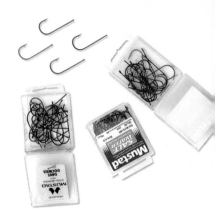

ABOVE: Hooks are available in packets or as shown here in boxes. The label will tell you what size and make the hook is.

wire hooks in particular will deteriorate when damp. Carry a sharpening stone in your tackle box and remember to check your hooks for damage when fishing over rough ground.

Weights

The weight you fix to the end of your trace will largely depend on how far you want to cast or how strong the tide is. There are many designs of lead, and each has its own special use. Some of the more common types are as follows: standard swivel bombs, available in sizes 2–6 oz (57–170 g), generally used from a pier when legering; torpedo leads, available in sizes 3–8 oz (85–227 g), also used from the pier or beach; and fixed-wire leads, available in sizes 4–8 oz (113–227 g). These are used to hold the tackle still on the bottom in a strong tide. Breakaway leads, available

RIGHT: These weights are specifically designed for beach fishing and uptiding. The wires fitted to the side of the lead act as an anchor for the bait when the tide is running. When pressure is applied to the lead, the wires fold back, enabling the lead to break free from the bottom either because a fish has been hooked or because the angler must cast again.

in sizes 3–8 oz (85–227 g), are widely used from beach, pier and rough ground. The wire grips are set in place before casting so that the bait is held still on the bottom. Once the angler pulls the lead, the grips break free and the lead is wound in.

When you are fishing over extremely rough ground it's a good idea to incorporate the use of a lead lift. This is a flight that is fitted above the lead and brings the lead up off the bottom as the line is being retrieved. Small ball leads and a tub of mixed split shot are a good addition to the shore angler's tackle box for mullet, mackerel, garfish and bass fishing. The ball leads can be used for float fishing and the shot for weighing down a live sandeel.

General Terminal Tackle

Other items the shore angler will need to carry are a selection of beads and sequins for trace-making. Beads or sequins can be added to the trace above the hook, and these will attract flatfish in particular. A good selection of swivels will be needed for joining traces to the mainline. Clip swivels are also needed for linking traces and leads. Split rings, both round and oval, are useful additions for linking traces to leads.

For running leger fishing, small sliding booms called zip sliders are handy to have in the tackle box. A selection of longer, fixed booms will be needed for paternoster traces. A sharp knife is essential for preparing bait and should be kept in a sheath for protection when not in use. This can also be used to cut line. It is a good idea to carry a pair of sharp nail clippers for cleaning off the ends of knot tails. A head torch is a good investment for night fishing because it can be worn around the head, leaving the hands free. However, for the more serious angler, purchasing a gas or liquid-fuel burning lamp will give much better lighting to work under. For the shore angler fishing with two rods, a rod stand or beach tripod will be needed. There are many modern stands on the market for the beach angler. The best are constructed from lightweight aluminium and are extremely light to carry, but very stable. They have a double head rest and double cup units to hold two rods securely. Most models are fitted with lamp-and-trace-holding hooks.

To carry all your terminal tackle, a good strong tackle box will be needed. Of the many available, the seat-box style seems to be the most popular. Not only will it provide waterproof protection and storage room for tackle, it will also double up as a seat for the angler. For protection from the worst of the winter weather, it will be worth investing in an umbrella or a specialist beach-buddy shelter unit, which will keep you dry and comfortable, especially if you are contemplating an all-night session.

ABOVE: The basic tools of the long-distance caster: a well-serviced reel with special spanners for maintaining it in good condition, and high quality shock leader material that will stand the strain of the weight when the cast is made.

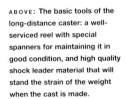

READY RIGS

For long sessions it is advisable to take along some food: sandwiches and chocolate for energy and a large flask or thermos full of hot soup, tea or coffee. The stainless steel unbreakable types, though more expensive, are a much better investment for the angler, especially if you are fishing from the rocks.

ABOVE: These pear-shaped leads are used for fishing a light rig over clean ground.

BELOW: Shown here is a selection of trace components. Each of the pieces shown can be used to make your own trace.

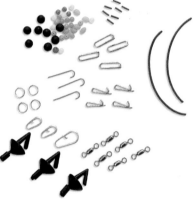

ABOVE: Small beads and swivels are essential for trace making.

LEFT: Ready-made rigs can be bought from the tackle shop. However, the beginner is advised to seek some advice to ensure the correct rig is purchased.

Beach Fishing

The open beach, with its pounding surf and golden sand, is a most inviting place for the angler to fish. There are many famous beach marks up and down the coast but probably the most famous is Chesil Beach, in Dorset. The Beach is more shingle than sand and as it enters the sea, its steep shingle banks drop away quickly into deep water. Many different species can be caught here, and this superb venue provides excellent sport for the sea angler all year round.

All beaches will have certain species that visit them during different times of the year. Flatfish of all kinds will move inshore and feed avidly on marine worms and crustaceans hiding in the sandy sea bed during the summer and autumn. They can be caught by the angler fishing with crab or worm bait on a running leger rig. Plaice and flounders are two species the angler can target at this time of year. During the summer months mackerel can also be caught in great numbers from the beach on brightly coloured traces of feathers. Summer evenings will draw rays into shallow water to hunt down sandeels and crabs over the sand. Often a whole fresh sandeel presented on a long-shanked hook will score with this species.

In winter cod is the prominent species to be caught from many of the beach marks along the coastline, particularly along the north coast. Fishing at night from the beach will often result in bigger cod being caught. A favourite method for the bigger cod is to fish with a lugworm

and squid cocktail on the hook. Hooks should be large and strong to accommodate a large bait and ensure a good hold once the cod is hooked.

In the autumn, after a storm, bass will be patrolling the surf in search of a free meal. This is a prime time to catch a specimen fish. The beaches of Dawlish and Teignmouth in south Devon regularly give up double-figure bass under these conditions. Fishing with a whole soft crab or using a large hook baited with razorfish are two successful methods to try. Don't cast too far though, as many of the bigger bass are just beyond the white foaming surf at a range of 30 yds (27 m) or less from the shore. Whiting and pouting figure highly in catches at night from the beach, and they can be caught easily by fishing at short range. A lot of anglers fish with a two- or three-hook trace baited with lugworm or squid to tempt these smaller fish.

TOP LEFT: This angler is using a beach tripod to keep the rods secure and steady.

ABOVE: An angler tails a smoothhound, hooked while fishing at distance from rocky ground. This is a species that can often be caught fishing from the shore.

Many of the country's fishing clubs hold beach competitions at night because the catches are often better than those obtained in daylight. Whichever species you choose to pursue and whatever time of year you do it, beach fishing is well worth a go.

Species to Catch from the Beach

Plaice, rays, bass, mackerel, whiting, dabs, cod, flounders, dogfish, soles and eels.

BELOW: A beach is an exposed and cold place in rough weather. It is wise to be properly dressed and equipped.

Pier Fishing

Piers are probably the first place most sea anglers get their grounding. High tide will bring many different species within casting range of the angler. In the summer months mackerel will be the main target during the day. They can be caught easily on light float tackle using mackerel strips or sand-eel. Garfish will also be present throughout the period from late spring to early autumn. Again, fishing with light float tackle baited with mackerel strip, with the float set at a shallow depth, will ensure good sport.

Piers are also a much-favoured night-fishing spot, and many species of sea fish will venture closer to the stone or wooden structure of a pier once the light begins to fade. Pollack and small pouting are prime candidates for a spot of fishing by lamplight, and it is said that a lamp hung from a pier shining out over the water will attract such species. Legering with ragworm close into the structure of the pier is the perfect tactic for pollack, coalfish and pouting. If there is enough light shining across the water from nearby street lamps or the promenade, a float can be used to good effect. Many of the modern sea floats actually have a fitting to accommodate a small chemical night light, known as a

starlight. Once the small tube of chemicals is slightly bent the liquids inside are triggered and mix together to create a bright light. The light can last for up to six hours and is a good way of detecting bites when float fishing at night. If legering at night, a starlight can also be fitted to the tip of the rod. When a bite occurs, the tip will bounce forward quickly, alerting the angler to the bite.

Another night-feeding species that can be caught close to the shore is the dogfish, especially in the late summer and early autumn. A nice fresh strip of mackerel on a running leger will sort out the bigger species. The occasional large bass is not out of the question, especially if fishing with mackerel or a whole soft crab bait after a storm. Larger bass are often alone and will follow prey fish in close to the shore at night. The pier is just the place for the bass to target an easy meal. Other species you may encounter are dabs and plaice if the pier is erected out over a sandy sea bed. A leger rig with a two-hook paternoster baited with cockles or squid is a method well worth trying.

Species to Catch from the Pier
Mackerel, dogfish, garfish, pollack, pouting, dabs, coalfish, whiting, bass, mullet, flounders, cod, plaice and eels.

ABOVE: Pier fishing is one of the sights of a British summer. Piers can provide the angler with some great fishing, and this angler has caught a small flatfish.

BELOW: Grey skies, gales and cold weather are bad news for the holidaymaker, but a combination of rough weather and high tides will bring many species close to the shore.

Rock and Rough Ground

Many of the bigger species of sea fish are to be found over rock or rough ground, as it is these marks that are usually associated with deeper water. When the tide is low the angler has a great opportunity to explore the terrain he will be fishing over when the tide turns.

Rock and rough-ground marks are natural larders, and the weedy gullies hold rich supplies of food for the bigger species. Fish such as bass, bull huss and the lesser-spotted dogfish will all visit these areas in the search for a meal at high tide. Walking the

ABOVE: **These anglers are fishing for bass and dogfish from a rock mark. Bass in particular will often venture into the rock gullies as the tide rises.**

BELOW: **This angler is casting his bait from a rock plateau.**

area at low tide will reveal every gully and trough created by the wash of the tide. It will also give the angler a valuable opportunity to pinpoint key marks such as deep gullies or clear areas on the rough ground.

Big cod and conger eels are two favourite species of the rough-ground angler. These can be pursued by day or night, with the latter being the more popular. From certain rough-ground marks these species can be caught at both low and high tides. With the tide high, fish will venture in closer and spend time delving through the weed and rock gullies. As the tide drops away they move back out into a secondary position, waiting for the tide to rise again. Find these secondary lairs, which are revealed on a low spring tide, and you can reap the rewards.

One of the main problems the sea angler faces when fishing over rough or rocky ground is loss of terminal tackle. This is usually caused by the hook or lead getting caught up on the rough sea bed. The tackle used must be strong enough to cope with these situations. A good strong rod of 12 ft (3.66 m) in length, matched with a robust reel and a line of 30 lb (13.6 kg) breaking strain is standard rough-ground fare. To keep losses to a minimum, expensive shop-bought leads can be replaced with a used spark plug from a car. These can easily be tied to the bottom of a trace.

Strong hooks and big baits are the key to catching and landing the bigger species likely to inhabit rough ground. Conger eels are a prime target and

can be tempted from their lairs with a nice, freshly cut mackerel flapper. This should be mounted up on a size 3/0 or 4/0 O'Shaughnessy hook on a trace of no less than 50 lb (22.68 kg). The lead (or spark plug) can be attached on what is called a rotten bottom. This is a length of low-breaking strain line, which will snap if the lead becomes caught. This is positioned above the bait on a running link. If, for any reason, the lead should become stuck on the bottom, the angler can pull for a break. This will jettison the lead, leaving the hooked conger still intact.

Species to Catch from Rock and Rough Ground

Bass, conger eels, bull huss, dogfish, cod and wrasse.

Estuary Fishing

Estuaries can provide some excellent opportunities for the shore angler, and for the flatfish enthusiast in particular they are key marks. Many species of fish will venture into the shelter of the estuary in search of food as the tide begins to flood. Mullet and flounder are probably the best known species associated with estuary fishing. Mullet can often be spotted entering the fresh water right at the top of the estuary. Stalking them with a light float rod and bread baits or even using a small spinner baited with ragworm can provide some entertaining sport.

On the south coast of Britain many bass are caught from estuary marks as they pursue the large shoals of sandeels that move into the estuary with the rising tide. In the lower reaches of the estuary, mackerel and pollack will spend time swimming around piers and jetties chasing shoals of brit. Both these species can be caught using float tactics, with a strip of mackerel or a sandeel as bait.

However, there is one species, the flounder, that is probably targeted more in the estuary than from any other venue. The flounder will feed freely on each tide. More associated with winter fishing, many estuaries offer flounder fishing for nearly all of the year. But in the months from mid-autumn to late winter, flounders are in peak condition, and the chances of a specimen fish are far greater. The Teign estuary in south Devon is an excellant example of a prime winter

flounder venue. Many of the big winter competitions are held here in December each year. It also holds the current British record for the species, with a fish weighing 5 lb 7 oz (2.66 kg). The Teign regularly produces flounder of 3 lb (1.36 kg) and over to the visiting shore angler.

To target flounder or any other species in the estuary, a 12 ft (3.66 m) beach rod with a medium action, matched with a reel holding 15 lb (6.8 kg) mainline is suitable. As the bottom of the estuary is usually soft mud and generally free of snags, a light hooklength of 10–12 lb (4.54–5.44 kg) can be used.

Flounder in particular can't resist a nice piece of fresh peeler crab used as bait. Present the crab bait on a size 1 or 1/0 fine-wire Aberdeen hook. If you go for some time without a bite

ABOVE: Take a close look at the estuary at low tide and you will be able to pick out the channels. Casting to these marks on a high tide will put you on the fish.

it often pays to move the baited rig a short distance along the bottom.

Quite often a bite will materialize as the bait re-settles. The flounder may have been watching and waiting for the bait to move and the movement tricks it into thinking the bait is escaping.

A good point for the shore angler to consider is that estuaries are a larder for fresh bait. It is well worth getting there as the tide is about to turn and flood again. Bait can be dug or collected and the angler can fish at the same time while the tide rises. The best times to fish in the estuary are usually one hour before the high tide and two hours after.

Species to Catch in the Estuary
Flounders, bass, mullet, mackerel, garfish and eels.

Making a Flatfish Rig

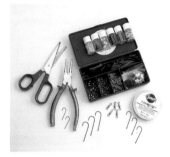

1 Beginner or experienced angler, you may prefer to make your own traces rather than buy them ready made. One of the easiest to make is an attractor rig for flatfish.

2 A 20 in (50 cm) length of memory-free line is used for the hooklength. A size 1/0 fine-wire Aberdeen hook is tied on securely to one end.

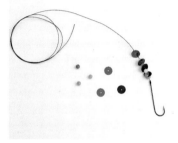

3 A few bright beads or sequins are threaded on to the line above the hook. These act as attractors and the bottom bead acts as a guard to stop the bait travelling up the hook.

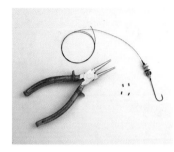

4 A very small crimp is now threaded on to the trace behind the array of beads and sequins. This is crimped in place with the aid of a pair of bottle-nosed pliers.

5 Once the crimp holding the beads is tightly in place, all that remains to do is to tie on a size 10 swivel at the other end of the hooklength and the flatfish rig is ready.

ABOVE: As well as making hooklengths for flatfish, with the right materials the sea angler can make many different variations of rigs. Here are just a few home-made rigs, made with Gemini components, which save the angler a good deal of money.

Spinning

When the sun is shining and its rays are penetrating the sea, a bright shiny spinner retrieved through the clear blue water can be a very effective way of catching fish. Mackerel, bass and pollack can all be fooled into mistaking the spinner for a sandeel or fry. Spinning is a method mainly used during the summer months by the sea angler fishing from the shore. Fishing with a bright shiny spinner can account for big catches of mackerel from piers and jetties, and it is an equally effective method for catching school bass from the rocks.

There are many different patterns of spinners available and a wide variety of colours to choose from. To spin successfully the rod and reel must be light and well balanced. A spinning rod is usually of a soft to medium action, and is around 10 ft (3.05 m) in length. It is matched with a fixed-spool reel of medium size, loaded with 8–10 lb (3.63–4.54 kg) breaking strain line. The soft to medium action in the rod allows small spinners to be cast a great distance. It also helps to absorb some of the shock when a fish is hooked and is making its first dive.

Many of the popular patterns of spinners are heavy enough to cast by themselves and need no additional weight on the line. At the head of the spinner will be a small swivel which is tied directly to the main line from the rod. A good overhead cast will have the spinner zooming through the air and into the sea some 50 yds (46 m) out. Let the spinner sink down for a few seconds and then start to wind the reel handle to retrieve it. Sometimes a straightforward slow retrieve will be all that is needed to trigger a reaction from a passing fish. When the fishing is harder, try retrieving the spinner at different speeds and work the rod from side to side as you retrieve. This will cause the spinner to slow and quicken as it is darting from side to side. Working it in this manner will give the appearance of a distressed fish and therefore an easy target.

Spinning for bass from the rocks can be good sport, especially if they are present in any numbers. Bass caught on a spinner tend to be on the small side and are known as schoolies. Silver-coloured spinners are good patterns to use. Remember

though, small bass are now a protected species, and it is illegal to take them from the sea at a length of 14 in (35 cm) or less.

Patterns of Spinners to Try

Toby and Krill for bass. Use standard mackerel spinners for mackerel and pollack.

ABOVE: **A large and well conditioned bass caught by fishing with a plug. Next to it lie a variety of plugs available on the market, including one that resembles a mackerel.**

BELOW: **These anglers are spinning for bass at dawn from a rocky shore.**

General Float Fishing

Mackerel and garfish are two favourite targets for the float angler, especially during the summer. A pier rod, or better still a freshwater carp rod, can be used in conjunction with a small fixed-spool reel holding 8–10 lb (3.63–4.54 kg) line. Fishing with light, balanced tackle like this will maximize sport from the powerful fighting mackerel and the acrobatic garfish. Setting a medium-sized float at a shallow depth of say 4 ft (1.22 m) is a well-practised method for mackerel. The float is fixed to the line by first threading the line through a stop bead. The stop bead will slide up to a stop knot of power gum or an elastic band set at the depth required. A float is then put on the line by passing the line up through the centre of the float. Another bead is placed under the float and under this a ball lead heavy enough to cock the float, is positioned. Another bead is placed under the weight and then a swivel is tied on to the line. To this swivel a 12 in (30 cm) length of line is tied and a size 1 Aberdeen hook is tied at the bottom end. Bait the hook with a strip of sandeel or even mackerel and you should catch a good quantity of these fish should there be any in the immediate area.

Where there are mackerel the sea angler is also likely to encounter garfish. The garfish tends to feed on, or near the surface, and it often pays to fish one bait below the float and one bait above it. Using the same set-up described for the mackerel, simply add a separate snood above the float. The baited hook on this snood will sink just below the surface and will sit in prime position for the shallow-feeding garfish. For other species, such as pollack and wrasse, the float is usually a bit larger, and only one hook is used. The only difference is that it is fished at a deeper depth and different baits are used. When fishing for wrasse from the rocks or pier, try baiting up the hook with a whole soft-back crab. The smaller the crab the better as it will allow better hooking. For pollack or coalfish a ragworm bait is preferred, especially if you are fishing at night from the pier.

Species to Catch when Float Fishing

Bass, pollack, wrasse, coalfish, mackerel, garfish and mullet.

ABOVE: During the summer months mullet can be caught close to rocks, piers and jetties. Stalking this shy fish with a light floating line can be a very pleasant way of spending a summer's afternoon.

RIGHT: A float rig for mackerel fishing. This is a basic rig set up that can be used for many different situations when float fishing.

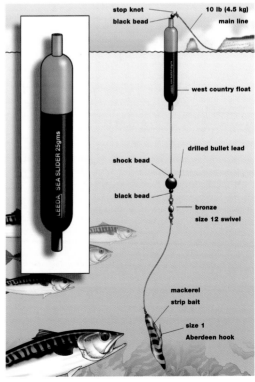

stop knot
black bead
10 lb (4.5 kg)
main line

west country float

LEEDA SEA SLIDER 25gms

drilled bullet lead
shock bead
black bead

bronze
size 12 swivel

mackerel
strip bait

size 1
Aberdeen hook

Shore Angling Rigs

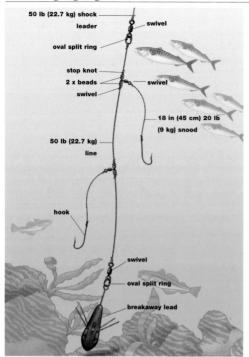

50 lb (22.7 kg) shock leader
swivel
oval split ring
stop knot
2 x beads — swivel
swivel
18 in (45 cm) 20 lb (9 kg) snood
50 lb (22.7 kg) line
hook
swivel
oval split ring
breakaway lead

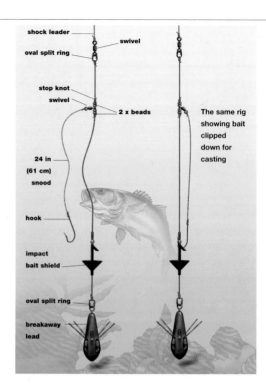

shock leader
swivel
oval split ring
stop knot
swivel
2 x beads
24 in (61 cm) snood
hook
impact bait shield
oval split ring
breakaway lead

The same rig showing bait clipped down for casting

ABOVE: Two-hook Paternoster

The two-hook paternoster is a popular rig to use from the shore when beach or pier fishing. Having two hooks set on the rig at a short distance apart gives the angler a chance to try two different types of bait at the same time. If one of the baits proves to be more popular than the other, it is a simple matter of changing the one that has failed. This rig is widely used when fishing for shoal fish such as whiting.

ABOVE RIGHT: One-hook Distance Rig

This rig is often used by the distance caster in search of cod and smoothhounds. The one-hook rig can be clipped down so it is able to be cast a considerable distance. Used in a strong tide the baited hook will sway in the tide and attract the fish. A bait shield is fitted to protect the bait on the cast.

RIGHT: Wishbone Rig

The wishbone rig is a firm favourite of the cod angler who is fishing at distance from the shore in a strong tide. The two-hook rig is able to run free, through a swivel and provides a "bolt hooking" effect when either of the hooks is taken by a large fish. The addition of a bait shield will allow delicate baits like lugworm to be cast great distances with minimal damage to the bait.

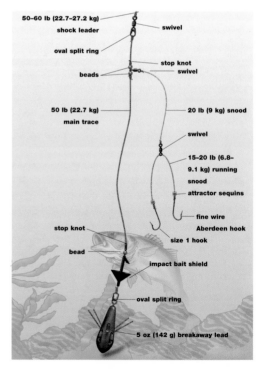

50–60 lb (22.7–27.2 kg) shock leader
swivel
oval split ring
stop knot
swivel
beads
50 lb (22.7 kg) main trace
20 lb (9 kg) snood
swivel
15–20 lb (6.8–9.1 kg) running snood
attractor sequins
fine wire Aberdeen hook
size 1 hook
stop knot
bead
impact bait shield
oval split ring
5 oz (142 g) breakaway lead

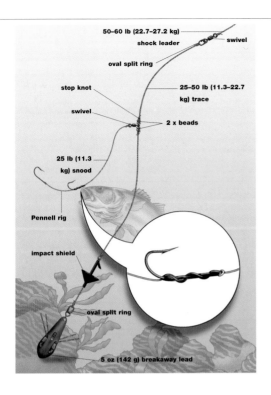

50–60 lb (22.7–27.2 kg)
shock leader — swivel
oval split ring
stop knot — 25–50 lb (11.3–22.7 kg) trace
swivel
2 x beads
25 lb (11.3 kg) snood
Pennell rig
impact shield
oval split ring
5 oz (142 g) breakaway lead

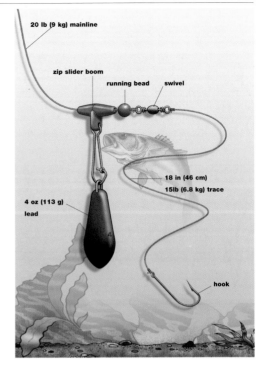

20 lb (9 kg) mainline
zip slider boom
running bead — swivel
18 in (46 cm)
15lb (6.8 kg) trace
4 oz (113 g) lead
hook

ABOVE: The Pennell Rig

This is a well-used rig when fishing for bigger species like bass, dogfish, cod and smoothhounds. The addition of the second hook on the snood allows the use of a bigger bait. Whole calamari squid can be mounted up to imitate a live bait when bass fishing. For dogfish, a side of mackerel can be mounted on both hooks, offering a large treat to tempt a take.

ABOVE RIGHT: Running Leger Rig

This rig is used when fishing over light shingle or sand. It is popular among sea anglers who are targeting flatfish, such as plaice or flounder. Using a small sliding boom with a quick-release clip on it, allows the weight to be changed very quickly without having to break down the tackle. The small rubber bead on the trace below the boom acts as a shock absorber.

RIGHT: Rough-ground Rig

This rig is used when fishing over rough and rocky ground. It is widely used when fishing for conger, tope, rays and dogfish. A spark plug can be used as a weight to keep losses of tackle down to a minimum. Also a rotten bottom link is used at the lead to enable the angler to jettison the lead and break free from a snag without losing a hooked fish.

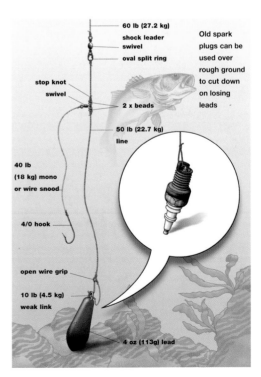

60 lb (27.2 kg) shock leader
swivel
oval split ring
Old spark plugs can be used over rough ground to cut down on losing leads
stop knot
swivel
2 x beads
50 lb (22.7 kg) line
40 lb (18 kg) mono or wire snood
4/0 hook
open wire grip
10 lb (4.5 kg) weak link
4 oz (113g) lead

Boat Fishing

The sea angler can improve his or her chances of catching bigger, and often more fish, by fishing from a boat. There are a host of different methods that open new gateways into the sport that in practical terms can be employed only from a boat. Fishing over sunken wrecks is a prime example, allowing the angler to present baits or lures directly over a fish-holding feature on the sea bed, something that is not possible when fishing from the shore.

ABOVE: Fishing from a boat brings the best chance to the angler of a big fish. This rod and reel combination is being pushed to the limit.

Fishing Afloat

The beauty of fishing afloat is that the marks and methods available are infinite, whereas fishing from the shore, pier or rocks is limited to how far you can cast and the make-up of the sea bed.

Of course, fishing afloat does have its drawbacks: you need a completely new set of tackle, including rods, reels and terminal gear, such as hooks, swivels and leads. There is also the problem of sea sickness, being stuck at sea on a boat that is rocking and rolling, and feeling or being sick is not the most pleasant of experiences.

Safety at sea is also an important issue, and under current laws every charter boat must conform to strict safety codes. These include having enough quality life jackets and life rafts on board, as well as a spare ship-to-shore radio, a comprehensive first aid kit and sufficient emergency flares. Remember if you do take to the open sea in a boat, always make sure you wear a life jacket. No amount of big fish is worth risking your life for. If you do not own your own boat it is possible to select a trip aboard a boat owned by a professional skipper.

Cost is an important factor since many of the deep-sea wrecking trips are more expensive than a charter hire. This is due to the amount of time and fuel the skipper will need to use to get you and other anglers out to the deeper water marks and on to the fish. An average price for chartering a good boat, including bait, is around £35 for a day's fishing. This may sound expensive, but when you come home completely exhausted with enough fish to fill up your freezer, it will seem worthwhile. It pays to shop around and ask for advice at your local tackle shop. Several sea angling clubs arrange their own trips, and it is good to be a member of an active club as there will always be the chance of a good day out at sea in the company of friends.

The last and most important factor when boat fishing is the weather. Unlike shore angling, fishing from a boat is governed by the wind. A force six wind is considered to be the strongest that can be fished in for safety and comfort. In some areas the wind direction also plays a vital part, and a force four easterly may be totally unfishable at one mark, whereas a force six northerly is fishable.

Boat Rods

There are numerous rods available for boat fishing, but there are really only three or four types you will need to be a successful all-round boat fisherman.

A good general-purpose boat rod for downtiding and wrecking is a 30 lb (13.6 kg) class model. These usually measure about 6-7 ft (1.83–2.13 m) and are excellent for fishing in deep water or strong tides for species such as cod, rays, turbot and other medium-sized fish. Many anglers who choose to use one rod for everything tend to pick the 30 lb (13.6 kg) class model. For the heavier species, such as conger eels, skate and sharks, it is recommended that you use either a 50 lb (22.68 kg) or 80 lb (36.39 kg) class boat rod, usually about 6-8 ft (1.83–2.44 m) in length. There are many available that have twin power ratings, such as 30–80 lb (13.6–36.29 kg) or 50–80 lb (22.68–36.29 kg) class, and these are usually the shorter, American-style, stand-up rods. The term stand-up means to stand up and fight your fish. Last, but by no means least, for the sporting angler, a good 12–20 lb (5.44–9.07 kg) class rod is ideal for a number of boat angling situations. These include drifting for cod and pollack over wrecks when using artificial eels and drifting for bass, plaice, turbot and brill over sand banks. Most of the modern rods on the market today are made from carbon fibre. The amount of carbon present in the rod will be reflected in the price tag. Some of the early models of boat rod are still available, and these are constructed from fibre glass. Many boat anglers still prefer to use the fibre glass models as they are often stronger than a budget-priced

carbon rod. Whichever you choose to use, make sure it can stand up to the work you expect it to accomplish. There is nothing worse than being miles out at sea with the wrong kind of equipment. If you are going boat fishing for the first time, many boat skippers will often supply tackle for the beginner. This is a good option to take before you invest in your own tackle. It will give you a better idea which rod and reel suit the style of boat fishing you are going to be doing.

Since most rods are designed to be used in conjunction with a multiplier reel, the rings on the rod will be in the upward facing position when you are fishing. Therefore, it is important to make sure that the rod has enough rings and that they are correctly spaced along the blank. Do this by attaching the reel and threading the line through the rings. You can then tie the end of the line to a heavy object and put the rod under pressure. The rings should prevent your line from touching the rod blank; if they do not, the rod either has too few rings or they are incorrectly spaced.

Boat Reels

Most boat anglers use multiplier reels because there are few, if any, fixed-spool reels that can stand the pressure and load that boat angling puts them under. There are three main multipliers that every good boat angler should own. First there is the 7000-sized multiplier, which can be used for general uptiding, drifting and downtiding. The second is the 6500-sized multiplier, which is perfect for light uptiding and all light-line fishing.

The last reel is a large 6/0-sized multiplier, capable of holding 300–500 yds (274–460 m) of 30 lb (13.6 kg) line. This is used for deep-water wreck fishing or downtiding and can also be used for conger eels and sharks.

There are two key points to look for when choosing a multiplier for boat angling. First of all, it must hold enough line for the type of fishing you intend to do. Second, and more importantly, the reel must have a smooth, powerful drag system that can be easily adjusted.

There are two types of drag: a star drag – a star-shaped disk found underneath the handle – or a lever drag usually found on the end plate of the reel. Most experienced boat anglers will choose a star-drag

ABOVE: A reel with a level-wind is suitable for novices.

ABOVE: This reel is better suited to big fish and deep water.

RIGHT: Make sure you match the correct reel to your rod.

ABOVE: This 7000-sized reel is ideal for uptiding.

multiplier for their general downtide and uptide reels, preferring a lever drag for bigger reels that are intended for playing big fish. The star drag is adjusted by turning the star either clockwise to apply more drag, or anti-clockwise to reduce it. A lever drag works by pushing the lever up for more drag or down for less. It is easier to adjust a lever drag when playing a big fish than a star drag. Whatever reel you choose, make sure it is matched to your rod to provide you with a balanced outfit.

LEFT: Take a mobile phone with you: you never know when you might need it.

OPPOSITE: Even when big fish are the quarry, a light, well-balanced boat outfit can give maximum sport.

Boat Terminal Tackle and Sundries

The average boat angler is likely to encounter many different species and marks and will need a wider variety of tackle than a shore angler will.

For instance, depending on where he or she wishes to fish regularly, a good selection of leads, including both plain and grip leads from 2 oz (57 gm) right up to 2 lb (0.91 kg), are needed. Sizes and patterns of hooks will also have to be varied, from the smallest size 2 Aberdeen-style for catching

ABOVE: Boat fishing line needs to be reliable and strong. It can be purchased on spools containing hundreds of yards (metres) of line.

dabs, black bream and soles right up to huge size 8/0 or 10/0 forged O'Shaughnessy hooks for conger eels, skate and sharks. Rods and reels have to be matched to the particular species or conditions, too, and this means carrying at least two or three different rods, plus the same number of reels loaded with different breaking strains of line. Line breaking strain will depend on the species sought.

As a rule, the angler will need two reels, one of which will be loaded with 30 lb (13.6 kg) class line and the other with 50 lb (22.68 kg) or even 80 lb (36.29 kg) breaking strain line. If you eventually drift into light-line lure fishing a reel loaded with 12–15 lb (5.44–6.8 kg) breaking strain line will allow some excellent sport for species

ABOVE: A variety of weights will be needed to cover different methods.

such as pollack and coalfish. Remember to go prepared, because there is nothing more frustrating than losing the fish of a lifetime because the line breaks. It is also a good idea to carry three or four spools of trace line for constructing the hooklength or trace. For instance, when fishing for rays, cod and smoothhounds a trace of around 40 lb (18.14 kg) breaking strain is needed, but for species such as pollack and bass the angler can use lighter lines between 12–20 lb (5.44–9.07 kg).

It is also advisable to arm yourself with a few ready-made conger traces fitted with large hooks. These can be purchased ready-tied to steel wire in most tackle shops. More experienced boat anglers often carry a selection of ready-made traces in a rig wallet.

ABOVE: Swivels of all sizes are used for tying traces and joining lines.

Unlike shore fishing, boat angling offers a wide diversity of methods, and to become a good boat angler you need to be aware of what these are and make sure you have the gear to practise them effectively. The main types of boat angling are uptiding, downtiding, sharking, wrecking, drifting and light-line angling, each of which requires a completely different set-up.

Until you actually start thinking about becoming a serious boat angler, it is hard to imagine the diversity of tackle and tactics used. For the average boat angler a selection of leads, from 2 oz (57 gm) to 2 lb (0.91 kg), should be sufficient. When you book your trip you will often find that many charter boat skippers will have a stock of bigger leads on board in case they are needed.

Other items to consider are hooks. The size and pattern of hook will depend very much on the species of fish you are after. Carry a wide

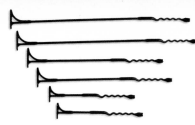

ABOVE: Booms come in all manner of lengths, and the longer types are usually used when fishing an artificial eel bait.

selection of sizes in different patterns; as time goes on you will get to use them. Swivels of various sizes and breaking strains together with a selection of beads will also be needed. Booms are widely used when fishing over deep water, and there are many different varieties available. Two of the most essential are the standard zip slider booms and the new, revolutionary Ziplock running booms. This type of boom is available in different lengths and will cope with all manner of rig presentations. It will also allow the angler to adjust the length of the trace without having to break down the terminal tackle.

Lures play a large part in boat angling, especially wreck fishing and drifting, so a good selection of pirks, artificial eels and jellyworms is essential. Probably the most widely practised form of lure fishing is the use of an artificial eel for pollack and cod when fishing over a wreck.

ABOVE: Both small and large hooks play their part in boat fishing.

No boat angler should leave the dock without a handful of rubber eels. The bigger the species you are after, the bigger the artificial eel you will need. These are fished on a long boom to hold a long flowing trace away from the mainline and are very effective. When buying artificial eels it sometimes pays to change the hook for a bigger, stronger pattern.

Another form of lure that will take its fair share of the catch is the pirk. A pirk is a chrome tube fitted with a large treble hook, and it resembles a

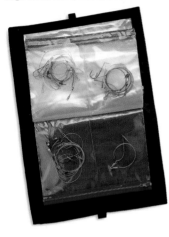

ABOVE: A rig wallet like this will protect your terminal tackle and traces.

smaller prey fish. Cod in particular fall foul to the pirk, and when baited with strips of mackerel or squid it is a deadly method for ling. Pirks can be made at home or bought in different weights from the tackle shop.

With all the bits of terminal tackle you are likely to take with you on a trip it is a good idea to invest in a tackle box for storing your kit. Some of the smaller items, like hooks, swivels and beads, should be stored in a rig wallet. Bigger items, like leads and other sundries, can be stored in a tackle box or small seat-box, which should also be waterproof and airtight. A good filleting knife for cutting bait and cleaning the catch is recommended, and if you are out at sea for long periods then a flask, preferably an unbreakable, stainless steel one, is essential.

When playing out a big fish over a wreck a butt pad can be a good investment. This allows the angler to balance the strain on the rod.

Clothing

For the shore angler clothing will be dictated by the weather. If the sun is shining and the air is warm a T-shirt, shorts and training shoes will be adequate. However, if you choose to fish in the colder months from beach or rock marks, it is important to wear suitable clothing to protect yourself from the elements and to keep you both warm and dry. A smock worn over a warm jumper will keep the warmth in on an autumn evening, but for the night angler it is advisable to wear a waterproof suit with a hood. If fishing from rocks or rough ground, investing in a flotation suit as worn by boat anglers is a sensible option. You can never predict the way of the sea, and it is better to be safe than sorry.

Footwear for the beach and rock angler needs to be waterproof and comfortable. Waders are fine for the short beach session and a strong pair of walking boots will support your ankles when rock hopping. Neoprene waders and chest waders are becoming more popular for the beach and rock angler, as they are light and waterproof and will keep you warm. Head wear in the form of a woolly hat and a pair of neoprene gloves for your hands will stop any heat escaping from the body.

Every licensed charter boat must have enough life jackets and life rafts for the number of passengers it is registered to carry. However, most boat anglers protect themselves by means of a flotation suit. Not only do flotation suits keep you warm during the colder weather, they also keep you dry. Each suit has enough buoyancy to keep even the heaviest angler afloat should he or she fall overboard. They come in a wide range of sizes, but most are either bright red or yellow in colour. Some manufacturers also incorporate special reflective

RIGHT: A flotation suit with a built-in buoyancy aid should always be worn when out boat fishing.

material to help the rescue services spot you at night, and most include a whistle of some sort in one of the pockets, so you can attract attention to yourself should you fall overboard and get swept away by the current.

You can buy a good flotation suit for a reasonable amount of money and it is a worthwhile investment to guarantee your safety. Most makes are available as either one-piece or two-piece suits, which come as a jacket and separate salopette trousers. There have been so many developments in recent years with regard to fabrics that you can now be both safe and warm without losing much of your mobility.

Other very useful items of boat fishing attire include fingerless neoprene gloves, woolly hats, thermal underwear, thick socks and Wellington boots, all of which help to keep you warm when the cold weather threatens. It is no fun being stuck out at sea when you are freezing cold, so make sure you prepare yourself well if you want to enjoy your boat fishing.

During the summer months it is important to wear some sort of hat, usually a baseball cap, and a decent pair of sunglasses. It is also important to wear high-level sun protection on exposed areas of skin – when you are out at sea you catch double the amount of sunshine because it reflects off the surface of the water. In addition, the wind dries your skin and increases the effects of exposure.

Charter Boat Fishing

Sea angling on board charter boats is by far the most popular form of boat angling in this country. Most coastal ports have their own charter boat fleet, and there are literally thousands to choose from.

All you have to do is book the boat for the day you require, which simply takes a telephone call. Most skippers will ask you for a small deposit. All you do then is telephone the skipper the night before your trip to make sure the weather is okay and will not keep you in port, and off you go.

Nearly all of the boats available are fully licensed and insured for having up to 12 anglers on board, but for comfort reasons it is better to fish with only eight or ten people.

Charter boats can offer a wide range of trips from three hours of mackerel fishing right up to 24-hour wrecking trips. However, the location of the port obviously has an effect on the fishing any charter boat can provide. The charter boat trip is often the first taste of boat fishing for many would-be boat anglers and it is a good way to get to know about the local inshore marks before contemplating a deep-water trip that could last for 24 hours. Do take note of what the skipper or his deck-hand is telling you. They will be thoroughly trained in the methods used – after all, it is their job.

ABOVE: The stern of the boat can often be the hot spot for catching fish over a wreck.

Most charter boat can get a 3 mile (4.83 km) licence from its local authority, which allows it to fish within these boundaries. Any charter boats that wish to fish further than three miles offshore have to be DOT approved. If the boat conforms to certain safety and technical standards, it will be issued with a licence that allows the crew to fish 20, 40 or 60 miles (32, 64, or 96 km) offshore. Check that the skipper of your chosen boat has this licence if you are planning a long-distance fishing trip.

Most skippers are, or have been, fishermen themselves and are only too pleased to take novices and show them the ropes. However, the best way to start boat fishing is to join a local sea-angling club. Here you can meet and make friends who will take you fishing with them and pass on their knowledge and experience in a practical manner.

Wreck Fishing

Fishing over a wreck is considered by many to be one of the most productive methods of sea angling. Often tons of fish can be hauled up from the depths by fishing over a deep-water wreck mark, using both baited hooks and lures.

The main species encountered when wreck fishing are cod, pollack, coalfish, bass, ling and conger eels. Methods vary from coast to coast, but the two main variations are either drifting with lures or baited feathers or anchoring uptide of the wreck and dropping baited traces downtide towards and into it.

As far as tackle is concerned, the species you are targeting will govern the type of gear you use and the weight of line and lure.

When you are fishing for conger eels, which is usually done while at anchor, a 50 lb (22.68 kg) class boat rod and suitable multiplier reel loaded with 50 lb (22.68 kg) mainline is required. Conger eels can grow in excess of 200 lb (90.72 kg), so sturdy tackle is a necessity. A whole mackerel bait with the backbone removed, is mounted on a large hook that is crimped to a wire trace.

Because the backbone of the mackerel has been removed, the two side fillets will flap around in the tidal flow. This presentation is known as a flapper bait, and it is extremely effective bottom fishing bait for catching conger eels.

When drifting over a wreck for cod, pollack or bass it is advisable to use a 20 lb (9.07 kg) or 30 lb (13.6 kg) class set-up. The lighter you go, the more sport you will have, but be careful not to under-gun yourself. Fishing on the drift is a method that allows the boat to move freely in the tidal flow. The skipper will position the boat in an uptide position and then cut the engine. The boat is then allowed to drift downtide, allowing the anglers on board to fish their lures or baits while the boat is on the move. This is a good way of catching pollack and bass when using artificial eels as a lure. The eel is presented on a long

ABOVE: A party of anglers boarding a charter boat for a day's fishing.

flowing trace attached to a boom. The longer the trace, the more natural the eel will look, and many anglers use a trace of anything up to 25 ft (7.62 m). As the boat moves downtide, the rhythm of the tide works the eel, making it look like the real thing. It is slowly retrieved to give added attraction, which often makes the fish attack it vigorously.

The method of pirking or jigging is well recognized as a good method for catching cod over wrecks. This is where a metal lure is worked over the wreck while the boat is drifting. The pirk is jigged up and down in the tide run, and the cod sees the pirk as a prey fish and attacks it. It often pays to tip the hooks of the pirk with squid

LEFT: The world-famous Eddystone eels are used all over the world for wreck and reef fishing. They are mainly taken by pollack and bass.

strips or mackerel fillet; this will give it added attraction. Another good method for catching cod and pollack is to use jellyworms on a long flowing trace, again while the boat is drifting. This is one of the more exciting

methods because you can usually feel the fish tapping away at the lure before it finally takes it. Jellyworms are a new breed of latex and rubber, worm-like lures from the United States. Generally, they are smaller in size than the big artificial eels, but they are just as productive and are fished in a similar manner.

Superbraids

The use of modern superbraids as a mainline has revolutionized the way sea anglers fish over wrecks. The lack of stretch allows the use of lighter leads and puts anglers in direct contact with the bait or lure so that they can feel a bite instantly. When using a braided line it is important not to strike at the fish too quickly. This can result in tearing the bait or lure from the fish's mouth. Because of the lack of stretch in braid the angler will be able to feel every little tap and pull as the fish mouths the bait. However, you should wait a second or two before you set the hook. Having fished with monofilament lines you will find the change to braid different to start off with. Once mastered, and with a little time and a bit of patience, the technique is not difficult: the use of braid can add a few extra fish to your catch.

How to Make a Conger Eel Trace

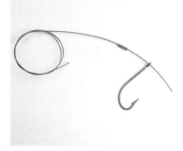

1 **When fishing for conger eels, a steel trace and large hook are used.** A steel trace can easily be made with little effort. You need 60 lb (27.3 kg) wire, size 6 or 8/0 hooks, some wire crimps and a pair of crimping pliers.

2 **Cut a length of wire and thread on a crimp, followed by the hook.** Then thread the wire back through the crimp, trapping the hook on the wire. Pull the crimp down tight to the eye of the hook.

RIGHT: A T-bar disgorger is a handy tool to have ready for removing the hook from fish with sharp teeth, such as big ling and conger eels.

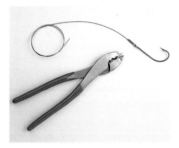

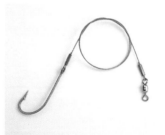

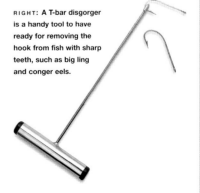

3 **Using the crimping pliers, apply enough pressure to close the crimp** right down, trapping the hook in position. Trim away any waste wire. At the other end of the trace a large swivel is crimped in place in the same manner and the wire trimmed as before. The trace is now complete.

4 **Do ensure that the crimps are absolutely tight and that neither** the hook nor swivel can slip free. This tackle is designed for big fish and you do not want to lose the largest fish you have ever hooked through badly made or faulty tackle. Store the completed trace in your rig wallet.

Shark Fishing

Fishing for shark is one of the more specialized branches of boat angling. Many boat anglers are not prepared to spend the time or money needed on a charter boat to target sharks successfully. Around the United Kingdom there are three main species of shark caught on rod and line: porbeagle, thresher and blue sharks. Other species are available, but they are few and far between. Of the three sharks that inhabit UK waters the blue is the most common. It can grow up to 200 lb (90.72 kg), but the average size is around 70–100 lb (31.75–45.36 kg).

Both the porbeagle and thresher sharks grow bigger, some may weigh as much as 500 lb (227 kg), but again the average size is much smaller, at around 100–200 lb (45.36–90.72 kg).

Strong tackle is a must when targeting big sharks. A good quality 50–80 lb (22.68–36.23 kg) class rod is needed, as is a suitable multiplier reel capable of holding several hundred yards (metres) of 50 lb (22.68 kg) mainline – a big shark can strip 200 yds (183 m) of line from a reel on its initial run in the blink of an eye.

Perhaps the most important item is the trace. A typical shark trace consists of around 6 ft (1.83 m) of 300–400 lb (136–181 kg) breaking strain wire joined to a further 10–15 ft (3.05–4.57 m) of 150–200lb (68–90.72 kg) wire via a quality barrel swivel. On the end there is usually a very strong hook, something like a size 10/0 or 12/0 O'Shaughnessy.

The Bait

Often a whole mackerel is suspended below the surface with the aid of a party balloon, which acts as a float. The usual set-up for a day's shark fishing involves no more than four anglers fishing at any one time. The four (or fewer) baits are suspended at different depths, usually from 50–60 ft (15.2–18.3 m) up to 10 ft (3.05 m) under the surface. Even though the trace may be 20 ft (6.1 m) long, the action of a drifting boat dragging the baits behind it sets the lines at an angle, so the bait ends up higher in the water. The drag is set on the reel, so that line can be taken easily, and the ratchet is engaged – a loud audible click that helps determine a run. There is nothing more exciting than hearing a ratchet scream as a shark picks up the bait and runs off with it.

At this point the angler should pick up the rod and disengage the ratchet. It is wise to let the fish run for 20 seconds or so before striking, and many experienced shark anglers will let the shark run until it stops, then strike when the shark starts its second run. Fishing for sharks is not for the faint-hearted as the fight can last for hours. For the bigger species the angler is usually strapped into a fighting chair, and the rod is attached to a harness to aid with leverage on the fish. Shark fishing takes time as the shark seizes line and then the angler gets it back, only to have the shark run again. Because of the sheer size of the shark, once it isunder control and alongside the boat, normally the trace is cut and it is allowed to swim free. There is no point in killing such a wonderful creature that provides so much sport.

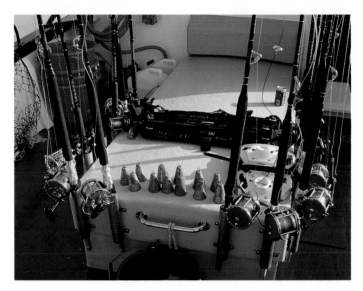

ABOVE: **A charter boat fully equipped for a day's shark fishing.**

ABOVE: **The successful and delighted angler boats a shark before release.**

BELOW: **A beaten shark is brought alongside the boat when the trace will be cut.**

Uptiding

The method of uptiding has proved to be one of the most successful ways of bait fishing over ground other than wrecks and reefs, such as sand or mud banks and rough ground. For many years boat anglers were limited to dropping their baits over the side of the boat, a practice commonly known as downtiding. This method is still the most popular today, but having the knowledge to be able to fish uptide has its advantages. It all started in the 1970s, when Bob Cox and John Rawle were experimenting in the River Thames. They discovered that by using a lead with wires protruding from the base they were able to anchor their baits uptide of the boat. This method of casting a baited rig uptide and away from the boat allows the angler to get outside the so-called "scare area", an area created by the disturbance of the anchor and waves slapping the hull of the boat.

Not only does it enable the angler to fish in an area away from the boat, it also often results in a much higher hook-up rate, because the fish often hook themselves.

The basic method involves casting a baited rig uptide and allowing it to hit the sea bed. The angler then pays off a few extra yards of line from the reel, which creates a bow of line in the tide. This ensures that even though the bait is anchored uptide, the angler's line still points downtide. When a fish picks up the bait, the resistance of the bow of line and the anchoring qualities of the lead drive the hook home into its mouth. A medium-sized fish often pulls the lead out of the sea bed when it gets hooked and a tell-tale bite is given as the fish, lead and trace trundle downtide. However, uptiding does have its limitations and is suitable only for marks in less than 100 ft (30.5 m) of water and those places that do not have strong tides. Standard uptide tackle usually consists of a 10 ft (3.05 m) rod with a fairly sensitive tip and a powerful middle and butt section. That length of the rod is needed so that the angler can cast the bait away from the boat. The main reason a sensitive tip is needed is so that the action of the waves on the boat doesn't "bounce" the lead out of the sea bed. Another reason the tip needs to be sensitive is so the angler can spot bites quickly.

ABOVE: This angler connects with his quarry while fishing uptide off a boat.

A multiplier reel suitable for casting, such as a 6500 or 7000 size, loaded with a minimum of 250 yds (229 m) of line is required. If you prefer to use a light-line approach of say, 12–15 lb (5.44–6.8 kg) class line then a shock leader will be required to take the initial shock of the cast. Even with lines up to 20 lb (9.07 kg) it is recommended that a leader of 30–35 lb (13.6–15.9 kg) be used. The strength of the tide will dictate the size of the lead you will need to use. In general, a breakaway lead or grip lead of 5–8 oz (142–227 gm) will do the job. The simplest rig for uptiding is a running leger, where the lead is

mounted on to the mainline so that it can run freely. This is usually done by means of a sliding boom, and there are a number of booms available specifically for use when uptiding in this way. After the boom has been placed on to the mainline it is followed by a small bead. A swivel is then tied on to the mainline to stop the lead running on to the hooklength. A hooklength made up of around 3 ft (0.9 m) of 30–40 lb (13.61–18.14 kg) breaking strain line is tied to the other end of this swivel.

The choice of style and size of hooks varies depending on the species the angler is targeting. In general, an Aberdeen or Viking pattern between sizes 3/0 to 6/0 is used.

Another popular rig is a sliding paternoster. This is made in exactly the same way, but the lead is attached to a length of line that is shorter than the hooklength, and instead of a boom, another swivel is used. When casting the rig, the angler needs to make sure the lead is outside the boat and that no other angler is in the way. The cast is then made away from the boat and uptide. As the flow of the tide increases, the angler may need to cast closer towards the anchor chain to reduce the amount of pressure that the force of the tide puts on the mainline, otherwise the lead will break free from the bottom.

Because casting is involved, soft baits, such as peeler crabs and

sandeels, may need to be whipped to the hook with fine bait elastic before casting to hold them in place.

When a bite is detected, the angler simply picks up the rod and starts to reel in quickly. There is no need to strike because the fish should already be hooked. At first, it may seem that the bite has been missed, but this is not so. The trace, lead and fish move back towards the angler with the tide. By the time the angler has taken up the slack line, the whole lot should be much nearer the boat. The angler will often connect with the fish only when all the slack line has been retrieved and a direct line and contact with the fish has been properly established.

It is important to wind in as quickly as possible until the weight of the fish is felt to prevent the fish from travelling too far downtide or even shaking the hook free. This is particularly so in fast-flowing tides.

ABOVE: The successful angler with a good cod weighing 7 lb (3.17 kg).

Boat Rigs

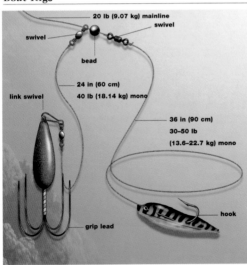

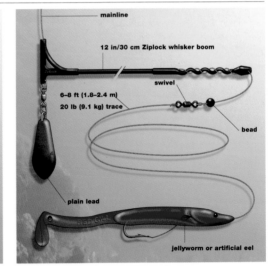

ABOVE: **Uptide Rig**
The uptide rig is employed by the boat angler who is targeting tope and cod. With the use of a grip lead, this rig can be anchored against the flow of the tide, allowing the bait to flap around in the current. Bigger species like tope are drawn to the lifelike bait. Big hooks and big baits are the key to catching those bigger species.

ABOVE RIGHT: **Artificial Eel Rig**
This is a popular presentation for catching large numbers of pollack and cod when fishing over a wreck. The skipper of the boat will use the tide to position the boat over the wreck. As the wreck appears on the screen of the fish finder, the angler will lower the eel down over the wreck. A long, flowing trace, as much as 25 ft (7.6 m) in length, is used to gain perfect presentation, allowing the rubber eel to behave in a lifelike fashion. The use of a Ziplock boom will ensure a tangle-free presentation, and a special retention clip allows the lead to slide down the line when a fish has been hooked. This means the angler can play the fish out on a short trace.

OPPOSITE: **Pirking Rig**
Often referred to as the "Killer" rig, this combination of pirk and artificial muppets always works when fishing for cod or pollack. The pirk, which is made from chrome piping, acts not only as an attractor but also as the weight needed to get the rig down deep and quickly. There is a large treble hook on the end of the pirk and two further hooks on the muppets, which are fished on traces above the pirk. Fish attracted to the silver glint of the pirk will often be caught on the muppets.

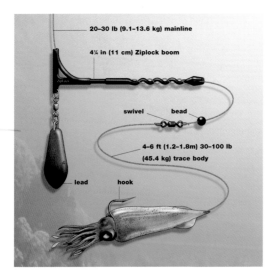

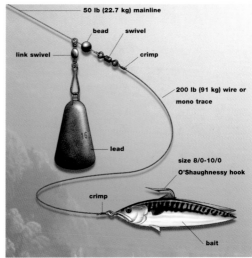

ABOVE: Downtide Rig

The downtide rig is used for fishing in the tidal current downtide of the boat. It is a good all-round rig for a variety of species. Pollack, coalfish, cod and bass can all be targeted with this rig. Hook and bait size will depend on the species being targeted. The use of a Ziplock boom ensures the bait is held well away from the mainline and lead as the rig is allowed to drift downtide, eliminating any tangles.

ABOVE: Conger Rig

This plain but efficient rig is used to target the large conger eels that inhabit many wrecks and rough-ground marks. A large hook and heavy lead ensure the bait is fished on the bottom, and strong line is used to cope with the powerful fight of a large eel. The hook snood will often be constructed of wire or very heavy gauge line as the conger has razor sharp teeth. Use of a lighter line will result in a lost eel.

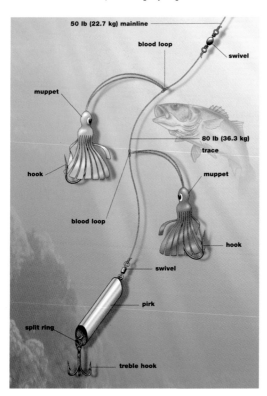

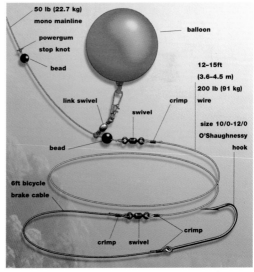

ABOVE: Shark Rig

When fishing for sharks it is common to present a drifting bait. This is done with the aid of a highly visible balloon. The balloon acts as a visual indicator and also as a carrying aid for the bait. It is picked up in the tidal current and drifts the bait away from the boat. When a shark picks up the bait, the balloon will pull free from the line. Strong tackle in the form of wire traces and large hooks are the order of the day for the shark angler.

Index

The publishers wish to thank the following individuals and suppliers for their contribution to the photography:

Dave Ellyatt
Drennan International Limited
Bocardo Court
Temple Road
Oxford OX4 2EX
Tel: (01865) 748989

Mike Ashpole
Ashpoles of Islington
Green Lanes
London N16
Tel: (020) 7226 6575

Brian Frattel
Farlows
5 Pall Mall
London SW1Y 5NP
Tel: (020) 7839 2423

Martin Ford
27 Willesden Avenue
Peterborough PE4 6EA
(01733) 322497

Lyn Rees
Shimano (UK) Ltd.
St. John's Court
Upper Forest Way
Enterprise Park
Swansea SA6 8QR
Tel: (01792) 791571

Fishing suppliers:
Relum
Carlton Park Industrial Estate
Kelfale
Saxmundham
IP17 2NL
(01728) 603271

PICTURE CREDITS
The publishers would like to thank the following people for their permission to reproduce pictures in this book:

Martin Ford and Dave Barham
– pp 1, 2, 4–5, 7 r, 20, 21 tr, 22 l, 24, 25 tl, 26 tl, 27 bl, 28, 29 cl, cr & br, 30, 31, 32 c, 34 bl, 35 c & b, 36 c, 38 tc & bl, 39, 40 tr, 42 tc & br, 46, 47, 48, 49 tc, 50, 51 tr, 54, 58, 60, 61, 62 tl.
John Wilson – pp 6, 7 tl, 29 tr.